MW01230913

Wicca For Beginners

Everything You Should Know about Witchcraft and Wiccan Beliefs Including Herbal & Moon Magic with Spells for Wiccan, Witches and Other Practitioners of Magic

LISA MAGIC

Table of Contents

Introduction

Wicca is a religion that many people do not understand because there are so many myths surrounding it that people have been taught and have not tried to learn the truth about. In this book, you will not only learn about what Wiccan is but what you need to know regarding herbal and moon magic.

As long as you approach Wicca with an open mind, you are not going to get yourself in trouble. Another thing that you have to remember is you cannot dabble with black magic or do anything that may harm someone else or yourself.

Throughout this book, you will learn about Wicca and how to do different spells involving herbs and moon magic. You will also learn other spells that you may want to use as you go about your journey in practicing your craft. You'll be surprised to learn that in many spells you will use herbs and a little bit of moon magic.

As someone who has been a practicing Wiccan for 10 years, I wanted to provide you with a glimpse of what you can do with your   magic.

Chapter 1: What is Wicca?

The first thing that you have to understand is that Wicca is not the worship of the devil, as many people believe. In fact, Wicca is a pagan religion that is based on the type of witchcraft that was developed in the 20th century. Gerald Gardner is credited as the one who brought the Wiccan religion to the public's attention in 1954.

Wicca is a spiritual system that is going to foster free-thought and the will of an individual while encouraging them to learn and understand the nature that will affirm the divinity that is in all living things.

Whenever you look at the Wiccan religion, you will discover that there is no central authority. Instead, it is based on traditional values and practices that Doreen Valiente and Gerald Gardner wrote about in the 1940s and 1950s while publishing their teachings so that their followers and many generations to come could read them and follow them.

As the years have progressed, there has been a multitude of generations that have come up with their own version of the Wiccan religion and it still continues to grow and evolve. Now you can find different sects and denominations inside of the Wiccan religion.

Being that this religion is decentralized, it is not uncommon that there are arguments over what the religion actually constitutes. These disputes are still happening today because some say that Wicca should be one way while others think it should be another.

However, there are a few traditions that can be seen in the Traditional British Wicca and those that follow this sect will focus on the teachings that Gardener wrote about, believing that the traditions are supposed to be observed by those following the Wiccan religion instead of the new traditions that some Wiccans follow.

How it Works

In the world that we live in it is hard to find someone who has not seen or read something that has a witch in it. There are a number of popular movies and books that are easy for us to access. The one most people think about is Harry Potter. When watching movies or reading books such as Harry Potter, it is easy to think that is how real witches work. However, this is not the case.

The meaning of Wicca is different for everyone depending on the sect that the witch falls into. There are some sects that worship the devil so that they can obtain the powers they want to do harm. But, in most cases, this is extremely far from the truth.

When you look back on the first humans that walked the earth, it was not uncommon to find that they worshipped gods and goddesses so they could have a healthy harvest and survive the winter.

Magic comes from chaos such as whenever someone becomes sick or there is a shortage of food. This is when spells are cast so the powers the gods possessed could be harnessed and used to put an end to the crisis. Most of the time, witches were females and they were considered to be healers who could use their magic to destroy or nurture the community they lived in based on what they believed.

It is because of the fact that witches can use their powers for good or bad that they tended to become isolated from others since people around them became scared of their powers and started to think that the witch would use their powers for evil against everyone. This is what started the witch hunts.

The History of Wicca

Wicca is part of the neopagan religions and is related to other neopagan religions that are based on witchcraft. Wicca first came around in the 12th century when a secret coven in England was developed so they could practice their religion based on the works of people like Margaret Murray.

Wicca became popular in the 1950s thanks to people such as Gerald Gardner who initiated the craft by a coven in 1939. The Gardner form of Wicca is known as the Gardnerian tradition and was spread around the world by Gardner himself, as well as his followers.

In the 1960s, there were new figures who rose to bring about their own form of religion under the Wiccan umbrella, such as Alex Sanders, Sybil Leek and many others who made organizations such as the Witchcraft Research Association. All of this occurred in a part of history when new religions were being moved to the United States so they did not have to be persecuted any longer for what it was that they believed in.

When the Wiccan religion came to the United States, it was adapted into new traditions and other sects of Wiccan that made sure the religion was never going to truly die out.

It was not until the 1970s that books were actually being published on the religion that encouraged others to join in the craft by describing the traditions and various other things that other people did not understand fully. As Wicca continued to rise, it became a major part of popular culture.

When the 1990s came around, there were historians that began to research the Wiccan religion and publish their findings so that others could know more about the religion.

Back in the 16th and 17th centuries, witch hunts took place which ended with around 100,000 people being killed after they were accused of being a witch because they supposedly worshiped the devil. Some historical documents even claim they ate children.

Some of the scholars who have researched the incidents have agreed that any of the victims of the witch hunts were incidents of hysteria that happened in villages that were not wealthy and were isolated. Those accused of being witches were not actually practicing anything that had to do with the religion. Not everyone believes this was the case though. Some scholars believe the victims really were practicing in the pagan religion.

A lot of Wiccans back in the early decades thought that there was a continuation of the witch cult and it was not until the 1980s that they began to see the witch cult was nothing more than a myth.

As previously mentioned, the Wiccan religion was founded sometime between 1921 and 1950. It is known as "the only full formed religion which England can be said to have given the world." The Wiccan religion actually was created from various other adaptations from religions that already existed along with some esoteric movements.

The Wiccan religion helped to prove that the people killed in the witch hunts were not worshipping Satan, but instead trying to survive in a world of pre-Christianity pagan religion. Several different historians have proven this fact through research. However, the most prominent advocate for this theory was Margaret Murry who wrote several books on the witch cult.

Debates

There are several debates that have occurred or are still occurring about where Wicca originally came from. If you look at Gardner's recalling in *Witchcraft Today*, it is a religion that managed to survive the witch cult and those who were persecuted in the witch trials.

Other theories say that the witch cult was planned along with all the trials so they can mostly be discredited. It is still very common for many Wiccans to claim they come from someone who survived the witch trials.

There are many theories on where Wicca came from originally and every sect in the Wiccan religion is going to believe in something different depending on the founder of that belief.
The one thing that has never changed in all of the decades that Wicca has been around is it is a very controversial topic and is the reason for much of the turmoil that is found in Wiccan religious communities.

Accepting the Wiccan Religion

When the religion first came around it was in a country that was dominated mostly by Christianity, which meant that it was not highly accepted that a new religion to be introduced.

Even today, many people, especially in the Christian religion, think that if someone is in the Wiccan religion they worship Satan. If that is not believed then it is believed that Wicca is a malevolent form of Satanism due to all the negative information that is out there about the craft. It does not help that many Wiccan covens and even individuals are secretive about practicing because they are scared of being persecuted for their faith.

Whenever someone comes out as Wiccan to their friends or family, it is commonly known as "coming out of the broom closet."

Doreen Valiente stated that "witches have little respect for the doctrines of the church, which they regard as a lot of man-made dogma." While this may be true for some, it is not true for all witches. There are some witches that are very tolerant of other religions and there are even some that believe in the Christian god. It is purely up to the witch and what they choose to believe in.

It is important to keep in mind that most of what is seen on television and in the movies about the Wiccan religion is not going to be accurate. So, when you are trying to choose if Wiccan is right for you, remember to try and look at the facts and not make your decision based on what has been seen on a screen.

In 1986, a legal decision was made to try and get the Wiccan religion validated as an actual religion. Despite this decision, and many other legal decisions, Wiccans are still having to fight politics and other religious organizations. One of these oppositions came from president George Bush because he did not believe that Wicca was a true religion and therefore it should not be recognized as one.

The Department of Veterans Affairs had a legal dispute in 2007 that made it to the stage where the pentagram can be added to the markers and plaques that are made in honor of the veterans that have died. The pentagram is now on the list of government recognized symbols for religion just like the cross is.

Even in Canada, the founding high priest and priestess of the Celeste coven, along with the founding elders for the church, were able to get the British government and the federal government to recognize Wiccan weddings and allow them to be performed in prisons and hospital chapels.

Types of Wiccans

As mentioned above, there are different sects in the Wiccan religion. While they all fall under the Wiccan religion, they believe in different things.

Gardnerian Wicca

A Gardnerian Wiccan is someone who follows the practices that were set into place by Gerald Gardner which is where the Gardnerian Wiccans came from. It is claimed that someone who is following in Gardner's footsteps is going to be following a religion that is straight from the New Forest Coven where Gardner first started his Wiccan journey.

A Gardnerian sect is going to typically have around thirteen members with a high priest or priestess. Any practices or rituals done by this sect are normally kept quiet from those that are not in the coven.

Alexandrian Wicca

The Alexandrian sect follows the teachings of Alex Sanders who was considered to be the king of the witches. His coven first began in the 1960s in the United Kingdom.

It is not hard to find ties to the Gardnerian Wiccans in the Alexandrian Wiccans as Sanders learned from Gardner before founding his own coven. These covens are usually more eclectic and have adopted the "if it works, use it" attitude.

Dianic Wicca

The Dianic Wiccans are more female centralized and focus on worshiping the goddesses rather than the gods. This sect is made up of several different cultures.

Witches in these covens typically focus on healing themselves from wounds that are left behind by men to reclaim their womanhood. Women in these covens are usually feminist, and they tend to celebrate the body of a woman rather than put it down.

Celtic

Just as the name suggests, this sect focuses on the Celtic religions and holidays.

The Celtic Wicca sect uses the same rituals and beliefs as most other Wiccans. Celtic Wiccans use the names of the Celtic gods and the seasonal festivals that are inside the Wiccan religion.

The Celtic Wiccans are seen as both Wiccan and a branch of Celtic Neopaganism. When you examine the Neopagan half, it ranges from eclectic to reconstructionist. On one end, Celtic Wiccan is eclectic while the non-historical forms are part of Celtic Reconstructionism.

Georgian

Founded by George Patterson in the 1970s, this sect is similar to the Gardnerian Wiccan sect except that it was founded in the United States rather than the United Kingdom. Many of the Georgian teachings come from a Celtic coven Patterson studied under.

Georgian Wiccan is eclectic and traditional as well. It is typically both males and females who have been initiated and been promoted to priesthood by the rites and rituals of the coven. Georgian Wiccans are oath bound. The lore of the tradition are only told to those that have been prepared properly. Even though the internet is a useful tool, it does not have all of the information required.

Believe it or not, Georgian Wicca is similar to Alexandrian and Gardnerian Wiccan. It's rituals are similar to those found in the books that are usually referred to as traditional Wicca.

Georgian Wiccan traditions are eclectic in multiple ways. It pulls from multiple sources including Celtic, Alexandrian and Gardnerian. It does not have a tie to any British traditional witchcraft coven. This is why it is usually referred to as a British traditional witchcraft derivative.

Discordianism

The Goddess Discordia is worshiped by this sect. Their holy book is called Principia Discordia. They believe that life cannot survive without chaos and order to balance out the universe. Discordianism says that the Greek goddess Eris is their central deity which is why they are often called Erisians. This religion places great stress on randomness, disagreement and chaos. The first rule of Discordianism is that there are no rules.

Is Wicca Right for You?

What it comes down to is: do you want to be part of the Wiccan religion? No one can say if it is right or wrong for you because it is based on your own beliefs. There are a few things you should consider to see if this is the proper religion for you:

1. You prefer natural stones to man-made ones.

2. You can recall your dreams without trying.

3. You are fond of collecting things that are found outside.

4. You would rather be outside than inside.

5. You feel like you have psychic abilities that come naturally.

These are not the only things that will help point you towards becoming a Wiccan. They are just a few indicators that will help show you the Wiccan faith is the proper religion for you.

Chapter 2: Practicing Wicca in Secret

It is understandable that you would want to hide the fact you are Wiccan because of how the outside world perceives it. However, when you are practicing in private, you have to be careful because it is hard to hide some of your spells.

The first thing you have to do is make sure that you are respecting anyone else's beliefs that you may living with. You do not want to go against their beliefs or upset them. Following from this, do not tell anyone that may communicate with your roommates. You will only want to talk to someone who you trust who knows they cannot bring it up to your roommates. If you cannot fully trust them, then you will end up being outed and that is not something you want to happen.

If you're wanting to work with stones, then one way you can hide that you are using them for magic is to say that you are interested in collecting stones because of how pretty they are.

If you are wanting a spell book, then you should get a journal that is going to keep people out of it. It is also not a bad idea to hide it somewhere like your closet or under your mattress. If you're a woman you can always get a journal that says "period tracker." If you're a man, you can try a similar tactic, only customize it so that others are not going to want to open it.

You can have herbs if you want. The best way to hide this is to have plants around that are going to make it seem less conspicuous.

You are not going to need a wand or herbs in order to be Wiccan. You also do not have to join a coven or cast spells. Remember that Wiccan is being one with nature and you can do this by going outside to meditate.

You can find a lot of information online (take some of it with a grain of salt). If you are sharing your laptop or tablet, make sure that you clear your search history. If you are printing out any information, place it in the journal you are hiding or you hide it somewhere else. Do not leave it out in the open for anyone to see! If you are not sure what to believe online, you can always go to your local bookstore and find books on Wicca or witchcraft. You can either read it there or buy it, take it home and hide it.

If you want an alter, make sure that you keep it small and put it away whenever you are done with it. If you are setting up an altar, it is not a bad idea to keep it as big as the top of your dresser or your desk. When you're done, place it in your closet or in the corner.

Do not hang up any symbols that would indicate that you are a practicing Wiccan. This also means do not get any jewelry or tattoos that will show you practice.

It will be hard for you to hide that you are a practicing Wiccan, but it can be done. Take the necessary steps to keep yourself protected and if you find that you need some support, there are support groups online that you can find and join.

Just remember that you are not alone.

Chapter 3: Witchcraft and Wiccan Beliefs and Rules

When you follow the Wiccan beliefs, you do not have to follow a particular set of beliefs. Instead, you will follow your own expectations. However, you should be advised that there are a few things that each sect of Wiccans believe in.

Beliefs

It is not required that you believe everything in the religion. Whether you are part of a cover or not, you are your own witch and you will be able to believe what it is that you want to believe without worrying about someone looking down on you.

Theology

For Wiccans, theology will cover agnostics, atheists, and theists and how they look at the religion as far as their archetypes and symbols go. Any Wiccans that are more theistic will have their own beliefs such as monotheists, polytheists, duotheistic, and pantheists.

Even though it does not matter what group the theist Wiccan falls in, they will still believe in a deity that predates Christianity. It is believed that Wicca predates Christianity by 28,000 years, if not more.

One of the most common forms of theological Wiccans that can be found are the duotheistic ones who believe in the Horned God and the Mother Goddess. How these deities are viewed depends on which sect the Wiccan falls in because every sect will have their own opinion. For instance, one sect views the Mother Goddess as the Moon Goddess and the Menstruating Goddess.

In 1959, Gerald Gardner wrote:

The Gods are real, not as persons, but as vehicles of power. Briefly, it may be explained that the personification of a particular type of cosmic energy in the form of a God or Goddess, carried out by believers and worshippers over many centuries, builds that God-form or magical image into a potent reality of the inner planes, and makes it a means by which the types of cosmic power may be contacted.

Afterlife

Just like theology, whatever you believe in when it comes to the afterlife will be completely up to you because it does not occupy a central place in the Wiccan religion. It is something that a few believe while others don't believe in it.

There are many Wiccans that believe if you do good in this life you are currently living while making the most of it, your next life will be good as well. However, it is more important for you to focus on what you are doing in this life because you never know what is going to happen in the next life.

On the other hand, there are some Wiccans that do not believe that there is an afterlife at all. Instead, they believe that your spirit will survive once your body has passed away and then it moves on to a higher plane. There is a religion found in Hawaii that says that the body has 3 souls that will survive after death. With that being said, not every Wiccan will believe in the afterlife, and some believe in reincarnation which means however you lived in this life will be based on how you come back in the next life. The more good you do in your current life, the better your life will be when you are reincarnated.

Magic

It is impossible for you to find Wiccans that do not believe in magic. Magic will play a manipulative force seen whenever you practice witchcraft.

Despite the fact that it is easy to find those that do not agree on the religion and see things differently, most will believe that magic is offered by ceremonial magicians.

Aleister Crowley once said "magic is the science and art of causing change to occur in conformity with will." On the other hand, MacGregor Mathers said "magic is the science of the control of the secret forces of nature."

As you can see, these two ceremonial magicians each believed that magic is something that can be controlled and can change something, whether it is with the will of the universe or the forces of nature.

Magic may have a different meaning for each Wiccan, but in the end it is the same thing. You will be releasing your energy out into the universe to make change happen.

You will see that the rule of 3 comes in here. Whatever you do, you will receive it threefold. So, you will want to stick to doing things that fall into the white magic category rather than black magic.

You may also see that there are two ways to spell the word magic. There is the traditional way, which is magic, or there is another way, which is magick. Magick is the spelling usually used by a witch that follows Crowley's footsteps and the way he believed in religion.

In 1970, Paul Huson stated:

The point [of magic in witchcraft] is to make the "bendable" world bend to your will... Unless you possess a rock-firm faith in your own powers and in the operability of your spell, you will not achieve the burning intensity of will and imagination which is requisite to make the magic work.

In other words, it is vital that you have faith in your own powers so that you can make the spell you are casting work properly.

Through your own research, you may discover that most spells can be done in a sacred circle that will cast a spell so that the spell works as it is supposed to. This will bring the change to the physical world that the caster would like to see.

Morality

Lady Gwen Thompson once said "bide the Wiccan laws ye must, in perfect love and perfect trust. Mind the Threefold Law ye should - three times bad and three times good...eight words the Wiccan Rede fulfill an it harm none, do what ye will."

Similar to the beliefs of Wiccans, there is no code that you must live by. However, there are rules that are known as the Wiccan Rede which is essentially the Wiccan version of the golden rule. The Wiccan Rede declares "an it harm none, do what ye will."

In simpler terms, the Wiccan Rede states that you can make whatever choices you want, but you must take responsibility for your actions, especially when it comes to harming yourself or others.

As mentioned above, the law of threefold return means that you will be messing with karma if you are trying to do something harmful to someone else. However, unlike karma, it will come back to you three times good or three times bad, depending on the spell you are casting.

Five Elements

Similar to magic, a lot of Wiccans believe in the five elements. Everyone knows what the 4 elements are (earth, wind, fire, water), but the 5th according to the Wiccan beliefs is spirit.

Rules

There are no set rules to the Wiccan religion, but there are a few rules that each Wiccan follows.

The rules and goals of the Wiccan religion have been touched on, but let's look into them a little more so that you can be one hundred percent sure that you understand them.

The Rule of Three

Ever mind the rule of three. Three times your acts return to thee. This lesson well, thou must learn. Thou only get what tee dost earn.

Just like the law of karma, whatever you put out into the universe is going to come back to you three fold so you need to be careful about what you are using your magic for or what you are saying.

Sometimes the rule of three is learned the hard way, but you are never going to get what you do not deserve despite what you have done. So, it is best to just do what you know is right and not do something that could end up coming back on you in a bad way.

Honor the Gods and Goddesses

They created life and they are there to help with the challenges that you are going to face every day.

Only allow the power to run through you in love, if it does not, then do not let it go through you.

Nothing should be done out of anger because that is when the rule of three is going to be invoked. No one needs to be harmed when it comes to doing magic because it is against the Wiccan beliefs.

This also means that you cannot make any vows to your gods or goddesses unless you are able to keep to them. If you cannot keep your vows, then you should not be making them since that is not a way of honoring your deity. It is similar to if you break a vow to your friends or family.

Do Not Bother Anyone Who is Not a Wiccan

It is understandable to be friends with people not in the religion, but you do not need to try and convert them like some other religions do.

Stick to the Vows That You Make to the Gods and Goddesses

Your word is your honor and if you do not do something that you say you are going to do, then it is going to come back on you. Any vow that you make should be honored so that the gods and goddesses do not turn their backs on you.

Do Not Use the Names of the Gods and Goddesses in Any Way Besides Love and Honor

This is very similar to the Christian's rule of do not take the Lord's name in vain. The gods and goddesses are meant to be honored and loved by all who believe in them and saying or using their name in an evil way will come back on you.

Do Not Sell Your Powers

Money should not be accepted in exchange for magic being done. You are the one who is doing the spell, therefore the consequences are going to come back on you.

There is no amount of money that is going to be worth being harmed three times what you do for someone else. Besides, you cannot control what other people are feeling when a spell is being performed nor can you control them wanting to harm someone else.

Know Your Craft

Never stop learning about the craft. Practice and never give up until you get it right. Nothing is going to go perfect the first time, but the more you practice, the better you are going to get.

Achieve Balance

Everything in the world has to be balanced and you should be balanced yourself. The more balance you have, the easier it is going to be for you to achieve your goals and keep your emotions under control when you are doing spells. Not only that, but you are going to be able to manage the good and the bad that is naturally inside of everyone.

Take Care of Yourself

Your body is a tool that was given to you by the gods and goddesses, so make sure that you take care of it to show how grateful you are for their gift.

Chapter 4: Wiccan Holidays

Just like any other religion, the Wiccan belief has its own holidays and festivals.

Major Festivals

Wheel of the Year

The wheel of the year is an annual cycle of festivals that are observed by most modern-day Wiccans. There are around eight festivals that can include the equinoxes and solstices on top of the other festivals that are observed.

Depending on the sect that you follow, you may have a different name and date for these festivals. Observing the cycle of the seasons is vital to many people, both in modern times and in the past. The only thing that has changed is the degree of celebration which will be based on various folk traditions.

It is said that Gerald Gardner took the word sabbat from a middle age term that was used for Jewish Shabbat.

Yule

Yule is known as the Midwinter Festival. This is a significant turning point in the yearly cycle because of the Stone Age. The sites of Newgrange and Stonehenge, both align during the solstice sunrise and sunset in order to help exemplify this turning point.

Whenever you look at the reversal of the sun's ebbing, you will notice that it symbolizes the rebirth of solar gods before the return of the fertile seasons.

Depending on where you are located or what sect you follow, you will celebrate this festival with gift giving, feasts or sacrifices. There are also wreaths made of greenery that are brought into the home during this festival.

Imboic

This is a festival that is on the first cross-quarter day that follows midwinter and will usually happen around the first of February. It is known as the first stirrings of spring.

It is during this time that you will do purification rituals that are also known as spring cleaning which help you get ready for the year's first signs of new life.

When you observe the Celtic Wiccans, you will notice that this festival is dedicated to the Goddess Brigid who is known as the daughter of Dagda.

The reclaiming traditions for witches is a time for pledges of the religion to rededicate themselves for the year. It is also the initiation for Dianic Wiccans.

Ostara

This is part of the spring equinox that typically falls sometime around the 21st of March. It has been said that this festival received its name from the Germanic goddess known as Eostre. Normally, you will see this festival celebrated around Easter or Passover. It is during this time that new crops are planted.

Beltane

Traditionally, this festival falls on the first day of summer in Ireland, but it is called the festival of Florais while celebrated in Germanic countries. There are various celebrations that take place during Beltane, such as maypole dancing and the crowning of the Queen of May.

Midsummer

This festival is also called Litha or Summer Solstice. This is one of the four solar holidays and is typically celebrated when the summer has reached its peak and the sun is shining for the longest day.

In the Wiccan belief, this festival follows Beltane and is followed by Lammas. There are some traditions, such as the Reckoning of Time, when a list is preserved with names for the twelve months, these names were created by the Anglo-Saxon.

Midsummer falls between June and July.

Lughnasadh

This is one of the three harvest festivals that take place. This holiday is marked by the celebration of baking bread in the shape of the gods and then consuming it in order to symbolize the sanctity and importance of the harvest. This celebration will depend on what practice you decide to follow.

The name Lammas implies that it is a grain-based festival. There is a feast to give thanks for bread and grain, which symbolizes the bringing in of the first fruits of the harvest.

Mabon

This is the second harvest festival and will be celebrated around Thanksgiving. This is a festival that is meant to recognize the fruit that the earth provides and they are shared to secure the blessing of the goddess and god during the winter months.

The word Mabon was coined by Aidan Kelly in the 1970s as a reference to Mabon ap Modron which was a Welsh mythological character.

Samhain

This festival is the perfect time for you to celebrate those that have passed before you. Festivities are usually time to pay respect to the ancestors and elders, pets, friends, family members, and other loved ones that have passed before you. Depending on what practice you follow will depend on if you are part of the festival that invites those to join the festivities or not. Many times, this is known as a festival of darkness because it is used to balance the festival of Beltane.

It is during this time that many believe that the veil between this world and the next are thinned which makes it easier for you to communicate with the dead. This is similar to Day of the Dead or Halloween.

Minor Festivals

Vali's Blot

This festival is celebrated around February 14th because it is a dedication to the god Vali and it is a celebration of love. This holiday is similar to Valentine's Day because it celebrates the love that is between two or more people.

Ancestor's Blot

Just as the name suggests, this is a celebration for your ancestors. This is another Germanic celebration that takes place around November 11th. This is a day to celebrate where you come from and what is to come.

Ancestors are extremely important in the Wiccan religion because they show you where you've been and where you are going. Your ancestors look out for you and keep you protected.

Yggdrasil Day

This day is celebrated on the 22nd of April and is the celebration of a world tree that goes by the name Yggdrasil. In reality, it is a celebration of all trees and nature. Remember, this is an earth-related religion which means that nature is a massive part of what you will practice.

Winterfinding

This is typically celebrated around mid-October and it marks the beginning of winter. This celebration will fall between Haustblot and Winternights. You will find that this festival will fall right after the harvest because it is your way of asking the gods to watch over you when the cold weather comes so that you can make it through the winter.

Summerfinding

Similar to Winterfinding, you will celebrate Summerfinding at the beginning of summer between Ostara and Walpurgisnight which is sometime during mid-April. You will celebrate new beginnings with this festival.

Chapter 5: Gods and Goddesses

The concept of a deity is you have someone to worship in the Wiccan religion just like everyone else does. These deities are said to be those that produced life and continue to ensure that life is given to everything in the world. You will see that these deities are similar to what God is considered in the Christian religion.

Major Deities

The major deities in the Wiccan religion can vary but will be similar and have something to do with nature. Most of the time, Wiccan's express their beliefs in their own deities with the writings that were completed by Doreen Valiente and Gerald Gardner.

Like everything else, the gods and goddesses will have a gender polarity but will both be equal so that everything is kept in perfect balance.

The Sun God and the Horned God

This is the polar opposite of the goddess. Most of the time, this god is seen as the horned god which links him to Cernunnos a Celtic god. However, in English folklore, he is called Herne the Hunter, in Greece he is Pan, in Rome he is Faunus and in India, he is Pashupati.

Gardner attributed this god to the witches of ancient times and was supported by Margaret Murry in his theory of the Pan-European religion which has sadly since been discredited.

The horns are considered a sign of male virility and any gods that have horns or antlers are usually found in the Wiccan religion. The green man is also linked to the horned god except he does not have horns.

Depending on the time of year, this god can have different personalities such as the Oak King or the Holly King, he has even been seen as the Sun King. The Sum god is usually found around the Lughnasadh sabbat.

Each aspect of the god are for the same god but there are some Wiccans believe they are separate deities.

You can find an extensive work on the Wiccan ideas of their god in *The Witches' God* written by Stewart and Janet Farrar.

Goddess/ Triple Goddess

Many times, the goddess is known as the Triple Goddess which means that she is the maiden, the crone and the mother. The mother goddess is the most important of the three.

Murry and Gardner claimed that there was an ancient goddess that was celebrated by the witches. Just like the horned god, the goddess helps to keep the balance in the Wiccan religion.

In classical Greece and Rome, the relationship between neopagan concepts and the triple goddess were disputed, although it is not disputed that the triple goddess came from ancient religions.

For instance, take Stymphalos. Hera was worshiped as a girl, grown up, and widowed. One of the most prominent triple goddesses was Diana which was equated to Hecate. Diana and Hecate were represented in triple form when they first started to be worshiped.

Neoplatonist philosopher Porphyry was one of the first to record that there were three parts to Hecate. He wrote:

The moon is Hekate, the symbol of her varying phases and of her power dependent on the phases. Wherefore her power appears in three forms, having as a symbol of the new moon the figure in the white robe and golden sandals and torches lighted: the basket, which she bares when she has mounted high, is the symbol of the cultivation of the crops, which she makes to grow up according to the increase of her light: and again the symbol of the full moon is the goddess of the brazen sandals.

Other Gods and Goddesses

The All

This deity is regarded as unknown and is not worshipped often. This deity is credited with organizing every principal within the world, which means that he is similar to the Tao or Atman.

Star Goddess

This is the universal pantheistic deity in the Wiccan religion. The star goddess is usually worshipped by the feminist Wiccan. She is also the one that is considered to have created the cosmos. The name Star Goddess comes from the charge of the goddess which is a sacred Wiccan text. Its origins come from the Feri tradition where the star goddess or Starhawk originated.

Lover God

This title is saved for the gods that have a goddess consort along with other lovers who are devoted to him. These gods are Pan, Cernunnos and Krishna.

Sacrificial Gods

This is a title that is given to those who have sacrificed to provide life for others. These deities are the Sun gods, green gods,   Jesus,   Osiris   and   Adonis.

Chapter 6: Book of Shadows

Everyone knows of the four elements: air, earth, wind and fire. However, in the Wiccan religion, there is a fifth element known as spirit. Here are how all of these elements come into play within the Wiccan religion.

The Five Elements

Air

Air is the representation of the mind and intelligence, as well as your communication and telepathy skills. It is expressed by tossing objects into the wind or with aromatherapy.
The following are attributed to the element:

- A masculine element.

- Its direction is east while its energy is projective.

- It is found in the upper left on the pentagram.

- Things that symbolize the air are clouds, feathers, vibrations and smoke.

- The gods and goddesses of air are Aradia, Cardea, Nuit, Urania, Enlil, Merawrim and Thoth.

- The spirits of the air are Sylphys, Fairies of the trees, and flowers.

- The time of day is dawn.

- The cycle of life is infancy.

- The colors are white, crimson and yellow.

- The zodiac signs are Aquarius, Libra and Gemini.

Fire

Fire is the representation of energy, inspiration and love. This is represented by the burning of objects or love spells. This is also an element of change and its magic represents itself. The following are attributed to the element:

- A masculine element

- Its direction is south with a projective energy.

- It is found on the lower right on the pentagram.

- Things that symbol the fire are things such as flame, lightning, volcanoes and rainbows.

- The gods and goddesses of air are Brigit, Hestia, Pele, Vesta, Angi, Horus, Prometheus and Vulcan.

- The spirits of the air are salamanders and firedrakes.

- The time of day is noon.

- The cycle of life is youth.

- The colors for air are red, crimson, white, orange and gold.

- The zodiac signs are Aries, Leo and Sagittarius.

Please note: be careful using this element. Do your rituals that deal with fire in an open space rather than the house.

Water

Water is for the representation of emotions and purification. It is represented by brewing water or pouring water over objects. The following are attributed to the element:

- A feminine element.

- Its direction is west with a receptive energy.

- It is found on the upper right of the pentagram.

- The symbols for water are oceans, rivers, springs and lakes.

- The goddess and gods for water are Aphrodite, Isis, Marianne, Mari, Tiamat, Yemaha, Dylan, Ea, Osiris, Neptune and Poseidon.

- The spirits are nymphs, mermaids, fairies of the ponds, lakes and streams.

- The time of day is twilight or dusk.

- And the cycle of life is maturity.

- The season is autumn.

- The colors for water are green, indigo, black, grey, turquoise and blue.

- The zodiac signs are Cancer, Scorpio and Pisces.

Earth

The earth element is for strength and stability. It is represented by burying objects and making images out of stone.
The following are attributed to the element:

- A feminine element.

- Its direction is north with a receptive energy.

- It is found on the lower left of the pentagram.

- Symbols for earth are rocks, soil, salt and clay.

- Gods and goddesses of the earth are Ceres, Demeter, Gaea, Mah, Mephtys, Persephone, Rhea, Adonis, Athos, Arawn, Cernunnos, Dionysus, Mardyk, Pan and Tammuz.

- The spirits are gnomes, trolls, and dwarfs.

- The cycle of life is aged.

- The season is winter.

- The colors are brown, black, green and yellow.

The Zodiac signs are Taurus, Virgo and Capricorn.

Spirit

This is the element that is for providing space and balance amongst all the elements. It is represented by a sense of joy and union.

The following are attributed to the element:

- A universal element.

- No direction.

- It is found on the upper part of the pentagram.

- The god and goddess of this are the Lady and the Horned God.

- The cycle of life is eternity.

- The season is the wheel of the year.

- The color is white.

Altar and Book of Shadows

Important tools of any Wiccan's rituals are going to be their altar and their book of shadows. Below we're going to go over what you'll need for your altar and how to set it up, as well as what your book of shadows "should be."

Altar Tools

This will be discussed in more detail in a later chapter.
Your altar is going to be where you conduct most of your rituals and where you "worship." There are a few tools that you're going to need to have on your altar even if you do not use them constantly.
Some of the things that you're going to want to make sure you have are:
1. The Athame (a ceremonial blade)

2. A bell

3. Candles for every direction

   - North: black, brown, green

   - South: orange or red

   - West: aqua or blue

   - Center: white, gold, silver or a god or goddess candle

- East: white or yellow

1. Pillar candles

2. A chalice

3. Images of your deities

4. A libation dish

5. Offerings

6. Pentacle

7. Salt water

8. Scent or feather

9. Stones or crystals

10. Your wand

You may also want to include your broom, cauldron, a working knife and a sword.

Your Book of Shadows

This is your bible essentially. There are not sacred texts for the Wiccan religion like there are in other religions. However, your book of shadows is going to include your spells and different things that you have gone through while on your journey.

In order to start your book of shadows, you're going to want to pick a book that you are comfortable working with. It can be a journal or it can be a spiral notebook. It is all a personal preference.

Make sure you label the book as well as set the purpose and energy of the book before you begin to write in it. On the first page, you're going to want your personal blessing before you go on with the rest of your book of shadows.

Here's how to set up your book:

- Book title and date

- Book blessing

- General index

- Sections

    o Magickal rules and principles

    o Goals and aspirations

    o Dream and divination records

    o Research

    o Classes and experiences

    o Spells, incantations and prayers

    o Rituals and ceremonies

    o Herbal remedies and potions

    o Closing thoughts

Chapter 7: An Intro to Witchcraft

What is Witchcraft?

Witchcraft is the belief in and practice of magical skills that are either exercised by an individual or a group of people. It is believed that witchcraft is a complex concept that varies between societies and cultures.

The term witchcraft should be used with caution depending on which culture you're talking about because it is not a cross-cultural term that means the same thing in each culture.

However, witchcraft can actually share a common ground when it comes to things such as sorcery, magic, superstition, paranormal, necromancy, shamanism, healing, possession, spiritualism, occult and even nature worship.

Witchcraft often plays a religious or medicinal role when it comes to societies or groups that believe in magic.

What Witchcraft is not

There are some misconceptions about witchcraft as there are with many things in different religions. These things are misunderstood mainly because people simply do not know anything about the religion or they have been taught it for so long that it is ingrained in their brain.

However, witchcraft is not all that everyone believes it to be. Here are some common misconceptions about witchcraft:

1. Witchcraft gives you ultimate power: This comes from Hollywood and the way they portray witchcraft in the movies that have witchcraft in them. While magic is real

and can be used by people, it will not give you the ability to do things such as:

   a. Call up cyclones on demand.

   b. Turn people into toads.

   c. Or any other childhood fantasy that we have had.

These kind of misconceptions come about when people only take what they know about the Wiccan religion from watching movies. Actually, practicing the religion is multitudes different than what you see on television and in the movies.

Sorry to say, you are not going to be lighting anyone on fire with your mind anytime soon.

Magic is more of a spiritual awareness in which you can work miracles by using your own energy. You are placing your energy out there into the universe to accomplish something.

2. <u>Wicca and Christianity are utterly opposed:</u> This belief mainly comes from the ancient prejudices that we see in the Old Testament due to people not understanding or being able to accept those that were different than them. Those who actually follow the teachings of the Christian god do not have a problem with anyone who follows another religion.

When you look at the Wiccan religion, there are a few similarities when it comes to the Christianity. Just like with every religion, there are pieces of all religions in one another. This is because each religion is slightly based on the others by taking the pieces that they like and evolving them to meet what they want to believe in.

3. <u>Witchcraft is Satanism:</u> This is probably one of the biggest misconceptions of witchcraft. When you look at it, Satan is not actually a Wiccan deity. The devil is a Christian construct that was used to reflect the fears of those in ancient times about those who practiced other religions.

In fact, Wiccans do not recognize Satan as a real at all. However, there are certain people in society who worship Satan and they are known as Satanists.

4. <u>Witchcraft is black magic:</u> Black magic is known as magic used to hurt someone or something. However, those in the Wiccan religion generally live by the rule of threefold and do not do harm to others. There are those that do practice negative magic in the Wiccan religion, but they are very few and far between.

5. <u>Witchcraft involves demonic possession:</u> The belief in demons is up to the individual. However, those in the Wiccan religion generally do not consort with demons, or any negative energies for that matter. Is it possible that some Wiccans actually do deal with demons? Yes. But, it is not part of the actual craft.

Science and Magic

Is there a tie between science and magic? Yes, there very possibly is. But it is not something that anyone can determine because the belief in magic all depends on the individual, not to mention how you consider magic.

However, you have to think about some of the things that we have been able to accomplish as a human race. Would we be able to do this without magic? This would be things such as flying, going to outer space, communicating over long distances, fighting diseases and much more.

So, is there a tie between the two? Who knows. Ultimately, it is up to you to decide if there is or not. No one can disprove the existence of magic because each person's magic is something different.

Ritual and Spell Work

Rituals and spell work are actually two very different things. Many people believe that they are the same thing because you can do spell work during a ritual, but they are actually very different. Here are some of the differences between the two:

- Spell work is a specific formula that you are going to use to shape your circumstances or in order to get a specific outcome. This usually takes you between space and time and is an act of creation.

- Spells are used to instruct, craft, weave, mold and swirl the different synchronicities.

- Spells are used to create something while embedding it to a life force within the living matrix.

- Spells add more energy to the energy web that surrounds us all.

- Rituals are the fostering of a connection between your mind, body and soul.

- Spells can be either simple or complex but are usually meant to touch something deep within your core.

- Rituals are prayers that are set in motion to make a physical gesture that merges within or even without but it is always something that integrates with your presence.

- Rituals are held in a space that helps you to maintain an internal state until it becomes a default space for you.

Ultimately, rituals are going to give you a structure that provides you with a safe space in which you can open up to your innermost self, whiles spells are going to transform you so you go from one state of consciousness and to another.

How to Become a Wiccan or a Witch

This is not something that you're going to wake up and decide that you're going to do one day. You are also not born with it. More often than not, it is something that you're going to accidentally come across one day unless you happen to have grown up with it being practiced around you.

The only way that you can actually become a Wiccan or witch is to do your research and decide if it is even the religion that is right for you. Make sure you understand the beliefs of the different practices and you believe in what the Wiccan faith is about.

Ultimately, the choice is yours to decide if you want to follow the Wiccan religion. Listen to your inner voice and see if you believe this is the right path for you. Do not let anyone pressure you into doing it because if you do then you may come to regret your decision. Not only that, but the ritual of becoming a Wiccan or witch is something that needs to be yours and yours alone.

It is important for you to design your ritual the way that you want it because you are dedicating yourself to the craft. You're going to want to make your dedication ritual one that you never regret.

Chapter 8: Tools You Can Use

Witches require the proper tools. Your alter tools do not have to be expensive or complicated. In fact, you can use what you have on hand. However, there are a few customary tools that you may want to get to fill out your alter.

Ritual tools are the tools that you will use to help with your rituals. It is important you know what the basic tools are and how you can use them.

This chapter will explain all of the altar tools and other tools that you should have on hand to help you better cast your spells.

Altar Tools

Each altar tool has a symbolic meaning. You should know the symbolic meaning of each tool so you are using it properly.

- Athame: A ritual knife that is one of the prime Wicca altar tools. An athame is typically black handled and will lie in to the east which is the direction that represents mind, choice and thought.

Athames do not have to be metal. You will be able to find ones that are made out of wood or carved from stone. It will not be used as a physical knife, but rather a symbolic one.

Athames hold the God (yang) energy. They will be used in directing energy and casting ritual circles as well as recalling them. They can also be used to cut energetic ties.

- Bell: Bells are said to be like the voice of the Goddess. Whenever you ring a bell it will bring the divine's attention to you and your attention to the divine. Bells that have lovely tones will call beautiful and healing energy to you. They can also be used to clean energy out of a space.

When you finish a ritual, it is a good idea to ring a bell. If there is any unwanted energy around you while you are performing a ritual, you can use a bell to get rid of it.

- Candles (directional): There should be one candle for every direction and each direction will be color coded. Candles are used in invoking and holding the powers of each direction.

  - *Center* - If you do not use a god or goddess candle, you can use white, gold or silver for your center candle

  - *North* - Black, brown or green

  - *West* - Blue or aqua

  - *South* - Red or orange

  - *East* - White or yellow

- Candles (God and Goddess): These are typically large pillar candles that are used to represent the God and Goddess. They are set on each side of the pentacle or somewhere near the center of the altar.

Some of the other options that you have are to place a large candle for the Great Goddess or even three (white, black and red) representing the Crone, the Mother, and the Maiden.
It will be up to you to place them, but be sure to place them somewhere where they are not going to drip on anything too delicate or catch fire. These candles will invoke the energies of the divine.

- Chalice: The chalice is one of the most important tools for your altar because it signifies the Mother Goddess. This is also known as a "yin" altar tool.

There are some Wiccans that place fancy bejeweled cups on their altar but that is not necessary. Any type of cup or wine glass will work fine, a bowl will work as well. As long as it can hold water and is rounded, it will work. Silver is always a good idea when you are placing something on your altar for the Goddess.

The chalice should be placed in the west which is the direction of the water. The Wiccan chalice is used for ceremonial drink, offering libations to the Divine.

- Deities: Any image or representation of the god and goddesses that you are worshipping is welcome to have a place on the altar. These images are not considered to be "altar tools," instead they are a reminder of the divinity. Statues of your gods and goddesses can hold actual vibrations of the divine. Your altar is a living temple where the divine will dwell.

- Libation dish: A bowl, dish or cup should be placed in the middle of your altar so you can place your offerings there. This can be your chalice or your cauldron. After your ritual, you will pour or bury your offerings in the earth or in living water so that they can be carried to the divine.

- Offerings: When honoring the divine with a gift you should bring them to the altar. Most of the time, flowers are kept on your altar as an offering, you can also use something that is beautiful and special or symbolic to you.

Offerings should not be anything that can be harmful in any way. Since the divine lives in all things, anything that is harmful to you will be harmful to the divine. Pragmatically, you will be placing your offerings in the earth later.

Offerings are usually overlooked in the Wiccan practices today. However, it is an aspect that can increase spiritual power and importance.

- Pentacle: This is a 5 point star that is surrounded by a circle and is usually placed in the middle of the altar. The pentacle is important because it offers protection and power.

- Saltwater: A small bowl that contains saltwater used for cleansing. This should also be placed near the middle of your altar or your chalice can hold the saltwater.

Water and salt are both considered purifying agents in the physical realm and the energetic realm. Saltwater also represents the energies tied to the earth and water as they unite.

- Scent or feather: The representation of air is usually marked by incense, essential oils, smudges, or a bird feather. This will go on the east side of your altar since the east represents air.

Sacred scents are used in cleansing the area's energy as well as calling in powers. It can also help you to shift consciousness. Feathers can be used to cleanse energy fields or spread incense or smudge smoke.

- Stones and crystals: For your earth element, you need to place stones or crystals. These will help bring you earth energy as well as help ground you. Crystals can help bring you energies that you may need to cast your spells.

- Wand: Wands are portable versions of brooms. The original theory was that one instrument could be used to perform all the purposes that are done by two today. Wands can be made up of any material that is natural. Wood is the most traditional because each wood is going to have unique powers, so you will want to choose the wood that is going to suit your needs.

Wands are also great for divination and channeling magical energy. You can cast and recall circles instead of using an athame. Your wand will go in the south because it represents yang.

Other Altar Tools

These are extra tools that should be kept near your altar but not necessarily on it.
- Broom: Brooms are not classified as altar tools, but they are great for when you have to get rid of any unwanted energy. You can keep your broom near your altar since it is too big to place on your altar.

- Cauldron: Most cauldrons are cast iron and have three legs. They come in every size. Cauldrons are handy to have around in case you have to burn items and that's why it is one of the most common tools to have on your altar.

Place incense charcoal at the bottom and sprinkle herbs and powders on it to create a pagan incense (Make sure you are careful when burning anything). Thanks to the legs on the cauldron, it should keep heat from the surface that it is standing on, but always make sure that it is. Also, try to keep anything flammable away from the top of the cauldron, especially your hair or your shirt sleeves!

Cauldrons can also hold any witch brews you may make. These brews will be magical spells in liquid form. This can range from saltwater to more complex spells.

- Working knife: This knife will be used to cut things and draw lines in the earth or runes on your candles. Most working knives will be white handled. The knife has to be distinctly different from the athame so that you are not confusing the two. Not every witch will have a knife as one of their altar tools, but it is a rather functional implement.

- Sword: Most people prefer to use a sword when it comes to casting in groups because of emotional or physical safety. The symbolic hostility that is in swords can be hard for sensitive people to cope with, especially when it comes to intimate situations such as rituals. Swords can be awkward when placed on an altar which is why some are kept near or under the altar to hold in the magical aura.

Other Ritual Tools

- Altar cloth: The altar cloth is optional but can be helpful. When you choose one that has the proper color or design, you will be setting the stage for the energy that flows around your altar. It will also help keep drip from scarring the top of your altar. You will want to choose a cloth that is not hard for you to remove wax from or will not be too expensive in the event that it gets ruined.

- Anything charged with magical energy: You can charge anything by placing it on your altar for a period of time, it is recommended that placing it on your altar for a full cycle of the moon is best. This can be spells, crystals, new altar tools, symbols of something you would like more of in your lif, or new deities statues.

- Book of shadows: If you have a book of shadows, it should be kept on your altar. This is one of the most important tools to be placed on your altar. However, if your altar is not private enough or you cannot keep it there because of space, it can be kept under your altar. Other books that you use for reference for spells or rituals can be kept under your altar. It is better to keep them close by rather than get up from your cast circle.

- Spells and spell casting materials: Any materials or spells should be kept under your altar if you are not using them when you first cast your circle.

- Songbooks: If you have a collection of songs or chants that you would like to use in your circle, keep them close by so you don't have to leave your circle.

- Tokens of helpers: Your altar is a great place for symbols and offerings to guides or special beings that help you throughout your magical journey.

Where to Find Altar Tools

You do not have to spend a lot of money on getting your altar tools. In fact, you can make your own tools or buy tools from other witches. If you do not want to do that, you can also find altar tools in alternative bookstores or in New Age shops.
Another option is to purchase them online. If you are doing that, there are Wicca altar starter kits that can be purchased online.

Chapter 9: Herbs You Can Use

Botanist have put in place a specific set of characteristics that set herbs apart from other plant life. For those that are cooks, healers or witches, the word herb includes any plant that can be useful to humans. This means trees, fruit, shrubs, flowers, vegetables and grass are considered herbs.

Interestingly enough, witches and herbalists use the word herb for any plant that has physical benefits to the body, including those that can be deadly such as belladonna and henbane. If you have any knowledge about herbs then you can understand that there is no plant that is good or bad, it just depends on what it is being used for in relation to the human body.

In the event that you are just starting out with herbal magic, ensure that you are heeding all warnings that regard toxic herbs because some of the old traditions use them. However, it is better to be safe than sorry, make sure you find an appropriate herbal substitute that is non-toxic for these recipes and spells.

Herbs That You Can Use in Spells

Herbs are vital for witchcraft because they can be used in a number of spells. Not only that, but they are required when you are doing herbal magic. In this chapter, you will see a list of some herbs you should keep around for your spells and what they can be used for.

- Camphor: A pain reliever, heals skin and burns. An herb sacred to the Goddess and can be used in full moon rituals as an offering to the Goddess. It purifies and promotes celibacy while heightening physical energy.

- Catnip: Helps to treat colds and reduce fevers. It can also aid in indigestion while curbing flatulence. It helps in strengthening the psychic bond that can be seen between humans and their animals. It is also used for courage, true love and lasting happiness.

- Cayenne: This is a great herb when it comes to first aid. It does not burn your skin or inner tissues even though it feels as if it is. Cayenne helps to coagulate the blood both internally or externally. If you are bleeding, it can be sprinkled on the bleeding cut to help it stop bleeding. It can also be used if you are suffering from heart disease.

- Chamomile: You can use chamomile to soothe your mind and body. It can be used as a sedative before you go to bed or as a pain reliever when placed in a compress. You can also use it for good luck or to change your luck.

- Clove: You can use this to soothe toothache pain or calm stomach pain. It also helps to banish hostility or negative energy while increasing personal gain.

- Coltsfoot: Relieves pain and is a cough and allergy suppressant. When used in spells it can help with prosperity and love.

- Comfrey: An extremely nutritious herb that soothes stomach pain, heals sprains, strains and fractures. It also can be used in protection spells.

- Diamiana: This herb is an aphrodisiac and improves digestion while relieving coughs. It can also be used in sex magic or for divination.

- <u>Devil's shoestring:</u> Protection and good luck.

- <u>Fennell:</u> Helps with digestion and can be chewed or placed in coffee. Helps to prevent curses while imparting strength and sexual virility.

- <u>Galangal root:</u> Cleanses your system internally and should be taken at the onset of a cold or flu. Can be used in sex magic, hex breaking and helps with psychic powers.

- <u>Garlic:</u> Good for hair and skin. Also helps to lower cholesterol and blood pressure. Can be used in magical healing and exorcisms.

- <u>Ginger:</u> A relaxing stimulant. Helps to settle stomach issues while inducing perspiration for sweating out a fever.

- <u>Ginseng:</u> Promotes longevity and can be used as an antidepressant. Can be used in love spells, healing spells and beauty spells.

- <u>Heal All:</u> This is an all-purpose healing herb. When gargled with cold water it can soothe a sore throat or can be used as a poultice for cuts and minor contusions. In spells, it can be used for success in gambling.

- <u>Hibiscus:</u> An antispasmodic that can also help to relieve hives as well as sweeten breath. When used in spells it can attract love. It can also be used for dream work and divination.

- <u>High John the Conqueror:</u> You will use this herb to conquer any situation that you may be faced with such as finding lost items or seeking protection.

- <u>Jasmine:</u> Calms nervous tics and can be used for snakebites. In spells, it can attract money and love. It can also be used to charge crystals or for moon magic.

- <u>Kava Kava:</u> A very powerful aphrodisiac and can help you with astral travel and protection when you are traveling.

- <u>Lavender:</u> This is almost an all-purpose herb. it can be used for stomach problems and it can also help you to find inner peace. It can also be used to relieve stress, find love, money or attract good spirits and faeries.

- <u>Lobelia:</u> This is an antispasmodic and anticonvulsive herb. It can also help to soothe any withdrawal symptoms you may be facing. Note that this is a poisonous herb and should only be used in small doses.

- <u>Mugwort:</u> An appetite stimulant and a digestive aid. You can use it for strength in traveling as well as clairvoyance or to boost power in your scrying tools.

- <u>Patchouli:</u> This herb will reverse spells and can be used in sex magic, divination and will help you to manifest and draw in money.

- <u>Pennyroyal:</u> You can repel insects with this herb and it can also be used in consecration rituals and exorcisms. Note that you should use this herb only in small doses.

- <u>Peppermint:</u> Can help to soothe heartburn and can also calm motion sickness. It will also promote peaceful sleep and boosts psychic abilities.

- <u>Plantain:</u> A blood detoxifier and also a treatment for poison ivy and bee stings. The juice of the leaves can be used on bites and stings. You can also make it into a tea or chew on the leaves.

- Raspberry leaf: Improves kidney function. It also helps with diarrhea and colds. It can help to promote peaceful sleep and can be used in protection and love spells.

- Rosemary: This is a nerve stimulant and helps to aid in memory and soothes headaches. You can also use it for protection, purification and healing.

- Rose Hips: This is a nutritious herb that is high in vitamin C. It can also be used as a mild laxative. When casting spells you can use it for good luck or to summon good spirits.

- Sage: You can use this as an antiperspirant. When gargled it can heal sores in your mouth and on your gums. You can also use it in your spells for wisdom, protection, money, healing and longevity.

- Sandalwood: You can use this as a poultice for bruises and contusions. You can also use it to stimulate sexual urges, healing spells and purification work.

- Skullcap: This is a tranquilizer and even an anti-insomniatic. It can help to relieve anxiety while promoting a peaceful feeling.

- St. John's Wort: Immune system booster and headache relief as well as a way to ease menstrual cramps. You can use it for protection, courage and exorcisms.

- Tonka beans: Can be used for good luck and attract material desires. Note that you should only use this externally.

- <u>Valerian:</u> A sleep aid and helps to treat nervous conditions. This is also an herb that is used in love magic and black magic.

- <u>Vervain:</u> This can be used for minor pains and arthritis. You can also use it in spells for protection, consecration and creativity.

Keep in mind that there are a lot of herbs that can be poisonous when taken in certain amounts. This is why you have to be extremely cautious when handling these herbs. Always make sure to consult a physician or even a horticulturist before you ingest something that you are not 100%   sure   of.

Chapter 10: Herbal Magic

Since the plants on Earth have been developed for millions of years, even before humans came around, it is fair to say that herbs are some of the oldest tools you can use for magic. For millennia, we have known that herbs have beneficial properties both physically and spiritually. There are many different plants that have been incorporated into the spells that healers, shame, and other medicine men and women used in the old days which is where herbal magic originated.

In the days before medicine was separated from magic, physical healing was usually accompanied by a ritual and a prayer. This was to ensure that the patient was treated with an herbal decoction along with a smudging ritual and incantation to the spirits so they could experience a speedy recovery.

In today's society, the ritual of enjoying herbal tea can have spiritual and emotional effects along with nutritional benefits. Combining healing and magical properties can make herbs powerful tools for modern magic. In fact, there was a study that showed patient practices for herbal magic to be the most rewarding form that a witch can discover.

Elemental Power of Plants

When you look at magical symbols, plants embody the power of 4 different Wiccan elements that work together to create and sustain life. First, they start out as seeds in the Earth where the minerals they need to grow can be found. From there, they interact with "fire" or sunlight, which helps to convert carbon dioxide into oxygen which affects the quality of the air we breath.

Air helps to foster more plants through the form of wind, which helps to stimulate the growth of stems and leaves which also helps in scattering seeds so the cycle can continue. Last but not least, all plants have to have water to live which is why plants play a crucial role in regulating the water cycles by purifying water and then moving it from the soil back into the atmosphere.

There is no better illustration that can show you how the classic Wiccan elements (earth, water, fire, air) can come together than to examine the cycle of a plant.

Plant Intelligence

Aristotle believed that plants had psyches, which is a word typically used when describing the quality of a human soul. Most Wiccans today would agree with his beliefs. In fact, there are some scientists that have begun to realize that plants have a consciousness.

Plants are able to communicate and interact with each other and other species. In the forest, trees and other plants have the ability to exchange information through an underground network of roots and fungus. This way of communicating allows them to exchange nutrients and help any plant that may have a shortage of nutrients at any point during the growing season. In other words, they are borrowing eggs from their neighbor while giving it back later with interest.

Plants are equipped to warn each other about any predators that may be nearby. So, if a leaf is nibbled on by an insect, then a chemical is released that will repel the insect while alerting the other plants to release their own chemicals.

These discoveries all demonstrate how intelligent Mother Earth is. No matter what part of the plant you are working with, you can tap into this magical energy when you are incorporating herbs into your spells.

Versatile Magic

When it comes to connecting with the earth's energy, nothing is going to beat working in a garden you plant with your own hands. Growing and harvesting your own herbs can keep you in touch with the Earth's powers as well as the elements. It also keeps you in touch with the role that insects and other animals play in the plant cycle. On top of that, gardening allows you to charge these tools with your own energy.

Herbs are one of the most versatile tools when it comes to hands-on magic. You can use them to create your own crafts like dream pillows, spell jars, sachets and other charms. There are some people who enjoy making their own oils and incense with their herbs which helps to add more magical power to their work.

If you do not want to make your own crafts, then you can also do "kitchen craft." This is where you make magical teas, potions, baked goods and tinctures.

Herbs are able to be used in many spells along with candle and crystal magic. Smudging is the ritual of burning dried herbs in order to purify or bless a space. It is one of the ancient traditions that has survived throughout the ages and made it into contemporary witchcraft.

Whenever you look at rituals, there are some Wiccan practitioners that use special herbs to mark their circle before they begin a Sabbat ritual. There are others that use herbs to honor their patron deities such as lemon balm which is sacred to the Roman goddess Diana.

Herb magic is incredibly practical and can be done with ingredients that are already in your kitchen!

Getting Started using Herbal Magic

The amount of information that you have access to on herbal magic can be overwhelming when you are first starting out. Just keep in mind that you do not have to be a master gardener or a botany expert to practice herbal magic. To get acquainted with the magical properties of herbs, you should only use one or two at a time to better build up your relationship with the energies that can be found in the plant world.

Some of the most popular magical herbs can be seen in the spice section of your favorite grocery store.

Chapter 11: Herbal Magic Spells

As you saw in the previous chapter, herbal magic primarily focuses on using herbs for your spells. In this chapter, you will see several herbal spells that you can do. Remember to be cautious when you use herbs since some of them can be dangerous when used wrong.

A Charm to Open Up to Love

If you have ever wanted to do a spell to bring new love into your life, then this is the place to start. Most people have a desire to attract a solid relationship but find that they have a blocked flow of energy when it comes to bringing love into their life, and they don't even realize that they are blocking their energy.

This herbal magic spell will figure out what is blocking you so that you can resolve any issues that are lurking under the surface. Be careful because this process can end up being uncomfortable emotionally. Just remember that when you release these blocks, it is going to be worth it because you will be able to find a solid relationship.

Charmed herbal sachets are perfect for you to carry around or wear. It is recommended that you use a small drawstring bag that is made of cotton or silk which can be purchased at a craft store. If you do not want to purchase one, then you can always sew your own.

In the event that you cannot get a hold of each herb on the ingredients list, use a greater quantity of the herbs that you are able to get a hold of.

Note: This spell also uses candle magic.

What you need:

- A pink candle

- 6 cloves (whole)

- A small bowl

- 1 tsp of dried mugwort

- 1 tbsp rose petals

- 1 tsp lemon balm

- ¼ c chamomile flowers

- 1 tsp St. John's Wort

What to do:
Once you have gathered all of the ingredients that you need, place them on your altar. Light your candle and take a few deep breaths to still your mind.
Move your bowl in front of you and mix your mugwort, St. John's Wort, lemon balm and chamomile together with your fingers. Make sure that you are gentle while mixing the ingredients together. From there pour your mixture into your sachet. Sprinkle the cloves in followed by the rose petals and finally close the sachet.
Hold your sachet in your hand and close your eyes. You should imagine your entire body is suffused with a white light that starts at your heart and moves outward. As you hold onto this vision for a while, allow a pink light to shine from your heart as it mingles with the white light. While you do this, recite the following spell (or something similar) at least three times.
As below, so above,
I release every unseen block to allow love in.

As above, as below,
My heart is healed and allows love to flow.
You should allow the candle to burn out on its own. Now you will keep the charm near you as often as possible which includes keeping it by your bed at night. Whenever you feel that its energy has fulfilled its purpose, you will bury the charm or you can open it and sprinkle the herbs back into the Earth.

All-Purpose Charm

This charm can be completed on any number of spells. For instance, take any herb that suits your purpose and tie it into a bundle that can be carried with you. Before you do that, you should place them on your altar. Small pouches can also be sewn with dried herbs placed in them. If you are seeking extra power, use fabric and ribbon in colors that are related to the intent of your spell.

A few examples for protection bundles can be made of garlic and parsley. You can use garlic and rosemary for purification or rosemary and marjoram for love.

To bless your herbs, say your own version of the following chant:

Enchanted herbs both brown and green.
Herbs for magic and the power be.
Goddess bless everything that I do.
For the good of all, I will do no harm.
With herbal spice, this spell is done.

Spell to Remove Bad Vibes

Take your kitchen salt and pour about an inch into a bowl. The next thing that you will do is squirt lemon juice onto the surface while repeating this chant.
Lemon juice and white salt
By mixing thee, I shall feel no bad vibes.
Remove despair and negativity
Goddess please, so shall it be.

Prosperity Spells

In a bowl mix together a teaspoon of cinnamon, half a cup of sugar, and a teaspoon of allspice. Next, you will pour it into a glass jar and screw the lid on lightly. You will empower the mixture using this charm. While you speak the charm, visualize your wish.
Sugar and spice and everything nice.
A bit of magic and a pinch of charm.
May my intent turn out as I want.

Prosperity Tea

Herbal tea has the ability to give you a financial boost. This spell can help bring you prosperity. You will most likely have all of these herbs in your kitchen and you may also find that you need to add some honey to sweeten your tea. Do not worry because it is not going to affect how well the spell works.
What you need:

- A sprinkle of ground flax

- A pinch of cinnamon

- A sprinkle of nutmeg

- A pinch of ginger (minced and fresh)

Boil a cup of water and add in all your ingredients. Stir them into the hot water and allow it to steep for around 10 minutes. As it steeps, you should visualize that you need extra money and envision how much better your life will be with the extra money. While the tea steeps, you will repeat a chant similar to the one below.

One coin here and one coin there.

Prosperity everywhere.

I need some wealth,

to fix my financial health

but I only need my share.

After the 10 minutes has passed, strain out the bits of ginger and other herbs. You can add some honey to the tea as mentioned earlier. Make sure to drink the whole cup before it gets too cold.

Bless This Kitchen

This charm can help you to bless your kitchen to enhance your powers.

What you need:

- Rough twine or string

- A large sprig of rosemary (fresh)

- Orange rind

- Bay leaf (whole)

You will tie your bay leaf and orange rind to the base of the rosemary. Make sure that you wrap it around enough times that it is not going to come apart. Once you've done this, you will want to hang it up somewhere in your kitchen that it can purify your space while bringing in positive energy.

Chapter 12: Moon Magic

Moon magic refers to any ritual that is performed using lunar magic. It will establish a connection between where the moon is positioned and the magic ritual being performed.

As you most likely know, the moon revolves around the earth. As it makes its revolutions, there are times when the earth comes between the sun and moon which is when the sun appears to be brighter than normal, these are called "full moon days."

On the other hand, when the sun comes between the earth and the moon, these are called "dark moon days." It is between these two points of a full and dark moon day that the moon will wane and wax which is known as the phases of the moon.

The moon is considered to be one of the most significant heavenly bodies when it comes to the Wiccan practices. Depending on the phase of the moon will depend on what role it plays in your rituals. This is because the energy levels of the moon will vary based on which phase the moon is currently in. The amount of energy that is found in the moon will be vital when it comes to performing your rituals. According to the most general principles of magic, the wax moon will be the time for new beginnings while the waning moon is a time to reflect and to alleviate negativity.

Moon Phases

Waxing

A waxing crescent moon is when the left side of the moon is darker than the right. There may be times that the moon is tipped so you are not sure if it is right or left that is dark. During the waxing moon, you can perform drawing, increasing and growth spells.

The waxing crescent will rise right after sunrise and then set just after sunset, it is only able to be seen in the night sky for a short period of time once the sun goes down.

Every night that the moon rises in the east, you will be able to see that the thickness of a waxing crescent will get bigger until the shape appears to be a half circle. This will be known as the first quarter or a waxing half moon. The left side will be dark and the right will be bright. You can continue the increasing, growth and drawing spells.

The waxing first quarter moon comes out around noon and does not set until around midnight.

From there the moon will appear to look as if it is pregnant because it will be round on the right side and have some darkness on the left side. This is known as a waxing gibbous moon. You are still going to be able to continue to do growth spells, increasing or drawing spells.

Waxing gibbous moons rise in the afternoon and set just before sunrise.

Full Moon

It takes around 14 days for the moon to completely grow or wax. The light from the moon will be reserved for light works and any dedication that you have to benevolent lunar deities. You can also use the full moon for prayers for peace and celebrations.

The full moon rises at sunset and sets at sunrise.

Waning Moon

Once the moon has gone through its 14 days of waxing, the entire process will reverse causing the moon to decrease in its size. After 3 days of appearing to be full, the moon will start to go dark on the right side. This is known as a waning gibbous moon and it will look as if it is perfectly round on the left side and then bulged on the right. This will be the time that you should do repelling, waning, reversing or decreasing spells.

A waning gibbous moon will rise early in the evening and set after sunrise.

Each night the moon rises in the east later and the thickness of the waning gibbous will get smaller until it appears that the moon is half a circle. This is called the last quarter moon and some call it the third quarter moon or a waning half moon. It will be dark on the right side and brighter on the left. You will want to continue to do any spells that have to do with reversing, decreasing, waning or repelling.

A waning last quarter moon will rise about midnight and set at noon.

While the shape continues to get small as the nights move on, the moon will become a waning crescent which means that the right side will be bigger than the left. You will want to continue repelling, waning, reversal or decreasing spells. This is also one of the most powerful times for you to remove curses or send back any evil to those that sent it to you.

A waning crescent moon will rise between midnight and dawn but will slowly fade once the sun has risen.

New Moon

Once the moon completely vanishes, it is known as the dark side of the moon or a new moon. This moon phase is strictly reserved for dark works and dedications done to dark deities. On new moon nights, there will not be any moon to see because it rises at sunrise and sets at sunset.

Waxing Moon (Again)

After up to 4 days, you will begin to see a small piece of the moon reappear in the sky at sunset. There are some people who call this the first crescent moon while others call it a Siva moon because of the Hindu god Siva. This is the time for you to start attraction, growth, drawing and waxing spells once again.

The first crescent moon will rise just after sunrise and set just after sunset.

From there, the moon will grow to the man in the moon type of crescent moon where you can continue your growth, attraction, waxing and drawing spells. From there, the cycle will start over where we started out.

How to Tell What Phase the Moon is In

To tell if the moon is waning or waxing, go outside when the sun is setting and look for the moon. If you cannot see the moon, then go out later and check again. You can also check during the day.

If you see the moon in the sky during the evening, the moon is in its waxing phase. Each night it will rise a little earlier and appear to be more full. Once the full moon rises, it will be able to be seen right as the sun sets.

If you cannot see the moon when the night falls but can be seen later in the night, or if you can see it during the day, then the moon is in its waning phase. Each day it will appear in the sky a little later and appear to be a little thinner.

A new moon will rise right when the sun does which means you cannot see it at all, no matter how hard you look.

Moon Energy

For every month of the year, there is a single full moon. However, if there are two full moons a month then it will be known as a blue moon. Every year there is at least one blue moon. Every month's full moon has a different name.

January: The January full moon is known as the Wolf Moon. This will be the time to shed any unwanted energy and cleanse yourself. The old year should be released so that a new energy can flow through you as the new year begins. This is the perfect time to release yourself from the past so you can start anew.

February: The full moon in February is known as the Ice

Moon. This is the perfect time for you to do some soul searching or to take a journey examining yourself.

March: The March moon is called the Worm Moon and this is a time to start new beginnings and explore new territories.

April: This moon is called the Growing Moon. You will want to gather and grow this month. It is also the perfect time to start things that you have been putting off.

May: The Hare moon is a time to nourish yourself emotionally, mentally and physically. You will need to pay attention to your needs and the needs of those you love.

June: The Mead Moon is the integration for the yin and yang that is inside all of us. This is the perfect time for attunement and understanding.

July: The July moon is called the Hay Moon which is the time that you should take to look at your life and think about any plans involving the future and look at the things that you should pay closer attention to.

August: The Corn Moon is the time to let go of any old emotional pain that is weighing you down. You should release it during this time and move on while making sure that you are more open and flexible.

September: The Harvest Moon is the time for you to start tying up any loose ends and trim up stray edges. Make sure you pay attention to any things that you have left undone. Start to examine your future with a clean slate and a clear conscience.

October: The Blood Moon is the time for you to build or start something that will flow into your new way of being as you get rid of old habits you no longer need.

November: The Snow Moon is the time for you to examine the things that bother you and reassess what is actually working for you in your life. If it isn't working, then it is time to get rid of it and find a new way to make your life go in the direction you want it to go.

December: The Cold moon is a time for you to cut away anything that you do not need in your life. Think of it as pruning a plant so that it can grow new shoots. You are not going to move forward if you have things that are weighing you down.

Chapter 13: Moon Magic Spells

You've learned that the moon has magical properties depending on what phase of the moon you are currently experiencing. In this chapter, you will learn about several different spells you can use by harnessing the power of the moon. Remember, some of these spells will require a specific phase of the moon in order to work.

Full Moon Money Spell

This is an extremely simple way for you to attract money. Ensure that you pass on some of the good fortune so that the flow of the universe is not interrupted.
What you need:

- Patchouli or Sandalwood oil (optional but is recommended)

- Green Candle

On the candle, you will need to write the names of each person that is taking place in the spell. If you want to anoint the candle with the oil that you chose, as you do this, recite a version of the following chant.
Now is the time that we weave our wills.
As the Gods and Goddesses reach down and lend us their strength,
we take it and place it to use.
We cast our energies out into the universe in order to create
our destinies as we wish them to be.

Now, you will light your candle and focus on the energies that are being sent into it so that they can be transformed and released through the smoke. The flames will be the power you need to do your bidding while you recite a version of this chant.

Full moon bright and full moon's light,
please grant me my wish this night.
Bring wealth into my life to stay,
so all my problems may melt away.
Allow money to come to me now
With harm to none,
so mote it be.

You will need to allow the candle to burn out on its own.

Moon Money Spell

This simple chant will help bring money into your life.
What you need:
- Paper money

This spell can be done from a full moon or new moon, you will need to go outside and identify the phase of the moon. Once you've done this, you will stand outside and place a dollar in each palm and repeat the following three times:

Moon moon, beautiful moon.
Fairer than any other star by far.
Moon moon, if it so be,
bring both money and wealth to me.
So mote it be.

Once you've done this, you may begin to notice that there is a change in your finances.

Moon Power

You can perform this spell outside or inside. You will be representing the moon with a piece of paper or a flower. In this incantation, the moon will be represented as a white swan. You should do this at a full moon to harness the energy of the moon.

What you need:

- Paper Moon (white) or flower (white)

- Bowl of water

Place your paper moon or flower into the bowl so that it is floating. Raise the bowl up towards the moon and repeat the following.

Hail to the white swan on the river. The present life, turner of the tide. Moving across the streams of life, all hail. Mother of new and old. To you, through you, this night I cling to the aura you present. Pure reflection, total in belief, touched by your mere presence. I am in awe of your power and the wisdom you hold. Praise to your power, the peace you give, my peace and my own power. I am strong. I praise. I bless.

Place the bowl on your altar and stand in silence, appreciating the power that the moon holds. This spell is an incantation to the moon which is why it is very simple. There are no other tools or skills needed except for the moon to be present. The water is a sacred tool to the moon which is why you offer it up to her because it belongs to her.

Snow Moon Spell

This is a simple spell that is going to awaken your new purpose in life.

What you need:

- A full moon in February (AKA Snow Moon)

- Violet candle

The full moon in February during Colonial American was called the Ice Moon because this was typically a time of fierce blizzards. Some people would call this moon the Quickening Moon because this was the time that nature started to reawaken. Despite the fact that the snow crocus would bloom, most of the land was still covered in snow.

During the Ice Moon, you will ask the Ice Moon to help you when it comes to making more positive changes in your life. Just like nature will awaken after winter has passed, you will also be able to awaken with a new calling.

When the Ice Moon is in the sky, you will need to declare your magical intentions to it. You will need to take your violet candle, which is your token of thanks, and light it as you begin to speak to the Ice Moon.

As the earth is covered in a sheet of white,
in icy splendor, you guard the night.
Allow me to make the changes, and let me be reborn.
As I plant this seed of magic, I will be transformed.
Allow your candle to burn out on its own.

Blood Moon Lunar Eclipse

This spell is going to call upon the Triple Goddess in order to grant you a wish or provide you with the power you need. This spell can only be done during a blood moon eclipse.

What you need:
- A calm mind (you should meditate before)

- Yourself

You should meditate as you take a ritual bath. As the bath water drains, you should invision all of the negativity from your day being washed down the drain. Once you're done, you should go outside a few moments before the eclipse and locate a place where you can see the moon clearly. After the moon is fully eclipsed, you should say:

I summon the Triple Goddess by all of her names, faces and forms. The Maiden, the Crown, and The Mother I summon and ask you to grant me a wish. I wish (insert your wish here and make sure that you are explicit). I thank you dear Triple Goddess. As I will, so mote it be.

Make sure to be careful about what you wish for.

Moon Water

What you need:
- Full moon

- Water

- Container to hold water

After the sun sets and the moon rises, take the container that you have chosen and fill it with water from a natural source. You can also use bottled spring water if you do not have any safe natural water sources close by.

Place the open container full of water outside and allow the moon's light to shine on it. Ask the Goddess to bless the water. The container should be left there as long as the moon is up. Once you're done, you will want to carefully close the container and keep it for any spells that require water. This can be done every full moon so you have a supply of freshly blessed water.

Full Moon Wishing Spell

This spell is good to use when you want to make sure that your wish will come true.

What you need:
- A glass of juice or wine

Under a full moon, you will need to go outside with your glass of juice or wine. Stare at the moon and tell her what it is that you wish for, you should visualize your wish coming true while you do. You need to be as specific about your wish and give as many details as humanly possible.

Whenever you have completed your wish, you will toast the moon goddess and repeat this chant:

Lunar goddess, look at me
This is the goblet that I offer to you
It is yours for everything that you do
Gracious one in silver hues.

After you're done, you will need to pour out your cup into the soil believing that your wish will be granted.

Moon Wishes

This spell will use candles as well as meditation. You can do this at both new and full moons so you can harness the moon's energy. By meditating before you go to bed, you will open yourself up to allowing your higher self to influence you.

What you need:

- A colored candle that represents your wish (it is recommended that it is in the color of your astrological sign)

- 5 white candles

Before you do this spell, you need to make sure your mind is free of clutter. It is also highly recommended that you meditate to ensure that you have clarified your wishes.

Next, place the white candles in the shape of a pentagram in a spot where they will burn safely. If you do not want to do that, you can light them according to the connecting lines found on the pentagram starting at the top.

While you do this, say the following incantation:

Moon above that glows so bright
guard my sleep so it may be deep this night
I pray to you with this one request

my life works out at my command.
You should allow the candles to burn for around half an hour before blowing them out and allowing yourself to go to sleep. When you wake up the next morning, light another candle and meditate while you think about what you wish for, this should take around 30 minutes. You need to spend some time visualizing what life is going to be like once your wish has been granted. This process should be repeated for 3 nights.
On the 4th morning, relight all of the candles and allow them to burn out as you listen to music that means something to you. In the last hour while the candles continue to burn, you will need to reconsider your wish and make any realistic adjustments necessary.

Full Moon Love Spell

This is a basic homemade spell that will increase your chances with the person of your choosing. You have to do this spell under a full moon.
What you need:
- Invoke the deity of your choice
- Meditation
- Pen
- Full moon
- Intent
- Casting circle
- Visualization
- Calling on the elements
- Paper
- Basil and cinnamon

- Stones (to increase your spell)

- Candle (pink)

You will need to focus your intent on what it is that you want. Why do you want the spell to be done? Make sure you cast your circle and call upon the elements while invoking your chosen deity that corresponds with romance or love.

Make sure to meditate with energy to charge your candle with that energy. At this point in time you should have cast your circle and called on the elements along with invoking your deity. Here is when you will anoint your candle with the herbs that you've gathered.

Light your candle and write your name and then the targets name on top of yours. Visualize that the flame holds your completed goal so that you can get with the person you want to be with. You should make a crystal grid around your candle to increase the energy flowing around you.

Once you've done this, repeat this chant:

It is on this blessed night
that I ask the goddess (the name of your goddess)
to unite these two souls in order to allow them to find
happiness
and romance.
May this romance warm the hearts of the couple and others with
the power that is inside these herbs and stones.
So mote it be.

Make sure that you thank your deity and leave an offering for them.

Chapter 14: Easy Spells for Beginners

Things to Consider Before Beginning

There are some things that you're going to want to consider before you even begin to do spells. Even without intending to, you can end up harming yourself or someone else because of the emotion that you have while practicing. It is important to remember that you need to be careful with each spell as well because each spell will have its negative effects if you do not do it properly.

Remember, do not cast any binding spells without being willing to accept the karma that will come your way. Do not cast any spells that will harm anyone without being willing to accept the karma. And do not cast any personal gain spells, rather cast spells that will give you the means to achieve what you're wanting to gain.

There are three questions you might want to consider before you begin any spell:

1. Have you tried everything to resolve the situation without using a spell or magic?

2. Is this spell going to harm someone else or bend someone's will to what you're wanting?

3. Are you prepared for anything that may come from doing this spell?

Beginner Love Spell

Everyone wants love, and it depends on what kind of love you are trying to attract that will determine how you're going to cast this spell. For this, we're just going to go over the simplest spell that we can find that any beginner should be able to do. What you need:

- Pen

- A pink candle

- White paper

The best time to do this is on a Friday night. **So,** when Friday night comes around, light your pink candle.

Using your favorite pen or favorite color, write your name and your lovers last name on the piece of paper. Next, draw a circle around the names and close your eyes in meditation so you can focus on the two of you together.

Next you're going to repeat these words three times:

Our fate is sealed, we are one. So mote it be. It is done!

Next you're going to watch your pink candle for about fifteen minutes all the while meditating on the person that you're wanting. If you can, you should meditate until your candle goes out.

If you use a larger candle than a tea candle, you can do the spell every night for seven nights making sure to meditate for fifteen minutes every night when you do the spell.

Beginner Prosperity/Money Spell

Money, who doesn't want it? We all do. In this section we will go over a basic money spell that you can try to see if you can raise your level of prosperity.

What you need:

- Athame or wand

- Dish of salt or earth

- Basil

- Chamomile

- Sage

- Cup of water

- Caldron and burning coals

The best time to do this spell is on a Sunday or Thursday during a waxing moon.

Cast your circle. Invite the lord or lady to your circle. Cast the herbs onto the burning charcoal while visualizing your goal. Next, sprinkle a few drops of water and salt upon the charcoals. While moving your wand or athame over your cauldron in a clockwise motion, use these words:

By the powers of air, fire, water, and earth. I
release this spell. I ask for Divine guidance as I seek
help this day. With harm to none, this spell be done.

Spend several moments in meditation as you imagine the smoke carrying the energy out of the circle and into the universe.

Thank your lord and lady for the assistance, release the circle and ground and center yourself.

Beginner Health Spell

Health is important to everyone. And just like everything else, there is a spell that can help you with your health. It is important that you are not using this spell to harm someone else's health because then you're going to have to deal with the law of threefold.

This spell is meant to help you with your own health.

There are multiple health spells that you can use, but this one is to alleviate headaches.

What you need:
- Glass of full moon water

- Clear quartz crystal

- Lavender scented candle

- One teaspoon lavender flowers

First you're going to want to dim the lights while taking a few moments to center yourself.

Boil a cup of full moon water until it reaches a full boil, drop in your lavender flowers and inhale the steam and aroma while saying :

Purple flowers heal my head; I will not take to my
bed. The pain will flee oh rising steam take the pain
with thee.

Then you're going to strain the liquid and sit while sipping the tea. Allow the warmth of the liquid to seep into our body while calming your headache.

When you are down to one sip, you're going to put the crystal over what is left and say:

Crystal bright, bring your shining light. Take this
pain to keep me sane. Right now I feel no mirth.
Your power is from the earth. Send this pain away
and make my day.

Now remove your crystal and place it over your third eye. Lie down a few moments and let the crystal absorb the pain.

Take the crystal to the sink and wash it under running water while watching your pain go down the drain.

Chapter 15: Protection Spells

Everyone wants to be safe, and with a protection spell, you are going to get the safety you are seeking. However, this is not the kind of protection that is going to stop intruders from coming in your front door if you leave it unlocked all the time. Make sure you are using some common sense in working your spell.

Sprinkling of Protection

What you need:
- Garlic powder (about a teaspoon)

- Salt (a handful)

First thing you do is mix the garlic and salt together (using garlic salt is not going to have the same effect so it should not be used). Next, you will take the mixture and put it around each threshold in your house. Make sure to get the windowsills as well. In doing this, you are going to be keeping all the negative energy out of the house.

Bury and Banish

Sometimes people come into our lives that we just need to get rid of. There is a spell that can help with that.
What you need:
- A black piece of paper (construction paper will work so you do not have to spend too much money)

Write down the name of the person on the paper. You do not have to be able to read it. Fold up the paper into the smallest square that you can get it into. Bury the paper in the ground somewhere outside. After you have it covered up, repeat this spell:

Into the ground
You cannot be found
You are not around
I cannot hear your sound.
Finally, step over the burial place of the paper. You should be able to see the person that you want to be rid of leave your life. After this spell, watch the person slowly fade out of your life.

Watch Your Step

This spell is meant to keep harm away from you as well as negative energy. This is a spell that will ensure that negative energy cannot cross the threshold of your home.

What you need:

- 1 garlic clove

- 3 pieces of broken glass

- 1 rusted nail or screw

Step outside your front door and dig a hole, it needs to be about six inches deep. Place all the items in the hole making sure that the garlic goes in last. Cover it up and stand on the small pile. Say this spell:

At this point,
all negativity in my life stops.

Do not remove the items from the hole as they are going to keep any negative influences away from your home.

Shield Spell

There is negative energy out there everywhere, and it is hard to avoid. But, you can shield yourself from it so that you no longer need to attract so much and carry it around with you.

What you need:

- A white candle

Cast your circle as you always should before you start a spell. Call upon your guides. Staring into the flame, visualize this flame wrapping around you and creating a shield from the negative energy that is floating around in the world. Say this incantation as you continue to stare at the fire:

Craft the spell in the fire.

Weave it well, weave it higher.

Weave it now of shining flame.

None shall come to hurt or maim.

None shall pass this fiery wall.

None shall pass, no! None at all!

Protecting Your Loved Ones

Your loved ones are those that you hold dear to your heart. They do not necessarily have to be family, they can be friends or anyone else that you want to protect. To make sure that no harm comes to those that you love, you can use this spell to put a barrier of protection around them and shield them from negativity and people that may be out to harm them.

What you need:

- A picture of your loved ones

- Candle (white)

- Protection incense

Light your candle and allow it to smoke. Placing the picture or pictures of your loved ones on your altar, put your white candle on top of them. Light the candle. Meditate and visualize a white light surrounding your loved ones with protection while reciting this spell.

O Goddess, shield my loved ones every day,

As they rest and as they play. Assist them to

Always smile bright, and keep them safe in

Your warm light. Protect them from evil

And from all they dread, for they are the ones

That I hold dear. I thank the Goddess for

Helping me. I trust in her aid, so mote it be.

Allow the candle to burn out on its own and go about as if your spell has already come to manifest in the physical world.

Chapter 16: Beauty Spells

We all want to be prettier, skinnier or whatever our goal is to feel better about ourselves. It can be hard to be happy with who we are because of the media and other outlets constantly telling us that we are not good enough. Magic is not going to make you supermodel beautiful overnight, but it can give you the boost you need to achieve your goal.

Melting Weight Loss Spell

There are not many individuals out there that can say they are happy with how much they weigh. If you are not happy with it, then you are going to want to change it. While the spell is not going to be the only thing that you can do, you are going to get some assistance from it to lose those stubborn pounds.
What you need:

- A brown candle

With a sharp object, carve how much you currently weigh at the top of your candle. At the bottom, you are going to carve what your goal weight is. Whenever you get ready to go to bed, light the candle. Allow the candle to burn for about fifteen minutes. As the candle whittles down because of the lightings, the closer to your goal you will get.

Grow Hair

Is your hair too short or you just want it longer? Without having to gather anything, you can say a spell that is going to help your hair to grow longer. Say the following three times a day:
My hair shall grow like weeds,
My energy will be like little seeds.

It will grow longer,
It will grow faster,
To my tailbone, it shall be.
This is my will,
So mote it be!

Weight Loss

What you need:

- A blue topaz stone

Charge your stone during a waning moon with this incantation:
Help me in my diet quest,
Bring me new strength and zest.
Take these extra pounds from me.
As I will, so mote it be.
Carry the stone with you and watch your weight drop.

Sleep Spell

Getting enough sleep is important to making you feel good inside and out. If you discover that you are having trouble sleeping, you can say this spell before you go to sleep so that you feel more relaxed and your sleep comes to you more easily.
Goddess above, queen of the night, help me sleep in
your healing light. Restful sleep come to me, relax
my body and let my mind be free. Grant me calm
and peace tonight and let me wake in the gods'
golden light.

Cleansing Bath

With a cleansing bath, you can wash away all the negativity that is attached to you and make yourself feel like a new person.

What you need:

- Lime (fresh)

- Candle (white)

- Rosemary

- Sea salt

Run yourself a warm bath. Add the sea salt into the water so that it has a chance to dissolve a little. Light your candle and place it next to the tub. Any artificial lights should be turned off.

Sit in the tub and try to relax, allowing all of your troubles to melt into the bath. As you relax, focus on the flame and think about yourself being renewed as you soak in the bath.

How long you stay in the bath is going to be a personal preference, you can soak in it as long as you want.

Before you can get out, you will need to knock the candle into the tub so that the flame goes out.

Refrain from using a towel to dry off, instead allow yourself to air dry, so you may want to stay in the bathroom if you have other people living in your home. It is wise to let others know that you are going to be taking time to spend in the bathroom if you only have one bathroom in the house. You are not going to want to be disturbed while you perform this spell.

Take your rosemary and the lime wedge rubbing them over your skin. Finally, drain the bath and visualize any impurities and troubles going down the drain with the water.

Chapter 17: Trouble Spells

Troubles tend to dominate our lives and when they do, we often tend to be forgetful and things in our lives tend to go downhill and then more troubles start. However, with some simple spells, we can at least get these troubles out of our mind so that we can continue with our lives and keep things going as they are supposed to.

Knot Your Troubles

It does not matter what trouble you are having, all you have to do is find the color that is best suited to what you are going through. You can look at the color chart that is located in the first chapter.
What you need:

- Yarn in the proper color (12 inches)

Hold the yarn taunt while you meditate on your problem. As you think about your problem, begin to tie knots in the string. Think of your problem being tied in knots as your fingers tie the knots.
Tie as many knots as you want or until you feel that you have tied enough. Bury the knotted rope once you are done to keep your problems away. Make sure you use a single color of string. One color per problem.

Clearing Up an Argument

Whenever you get into an argument with a friend or loved one, you may feel like there is something that is blocking you from making up with them. With this spell, you are going to be able to clear the air and move past it.
What you need:

- Candle (yellow)

- Paper envelope

- 1 bay leaf

Enscribe your name on one side of the envelope. Use the other side to write the name of the person you are fighting with. Put the bay leaf in the envelope and seal it shut. Light the candle as you hold the envelope over the flame, allowing it to burn. Ensure that you have a bowl of water to drop the paper into so that you do not burn your fingers.

Removing Anger

You are not going to have to set anything up for a ritual and you can teach this to other people because you do not need anything special.
What you need:

- A stone

Place the stone in your hand and visualize the anger that you are feeling moving through you and into the stone.
At that point in time, you will feel like all your anger is now sitting inside of the stone. Throw the stone away from you. It is best if you throw it into a body of water to ensure that the stone can become cleansed.
Repeat the following spell to ensure your anger has been removed:
Great guardians of the west
Who watch over the sea and ocean,
Let this anger disperse through space and time,
Make it disappear forever.
So mote it be.

Ending Heartbreak

Heartbreak is difficult to get over, especially when you really loved the person. But, if you cannot get over the heartbreak, you are going to be stuck in a place that is not good for your mental health. Therefore, you have to protect yourself and end the heartbreak so that you can move on with your life.

What you need:
- Cauldron

- Candles (one for every element)

- White sage (ground up)

- Rose incense

Cast your circle. Place your candles where they belong around the circle as they would appear on the pentacle. Light all your candles going around the circle. Now you can light your incense. Lastly, take the sage and burn it in the cauldron. Say the following incantation:

My fault it be not,
Forever he/she forgets me not,
He/she blames me for their inner strife
Left me heart broken with doubts of life.
My strength returned
His/her dominance slipped.
I will be my own person,
Strong, cleansed, and pure.
With harm to none
This spell be done.
This is my will
So mote it be.

Spirit Vanishing Spell

If there is an entity in your house that you no longer want there, you are going to have to banish it so that it knows that it is not wanted there.

While you have probably seen the television shows that depict a big elaborate process in getting rid of a spirit, it is nothing more than a show. You do not need anything but your voice to get rid of the spirit so that you can take charge of your house once more. There is no need for you to live your life in fear or with a spirit that you are not wanting in your life.

Stand in the middle of the chamber and speak these words three times in a row with conviction.

Evil spirit standing tall, it is time for you made your greatest fall.

Return to hell thou evil plight; I banish with this holy light!

Now go away and leave my sight and take with you this endless night!

Chapter 18: Luck Spells

Luck, we all need it, and it is something that is hard to come by. If we can get ourselves a little bit of luck, why do we not do it? This chapter is where you are going to find all of your luck spells.

Simple Wiccan Luck Spell

At times where you find one bad thing happening after another, you can use this spell in order to turn your luck around.

What you need:

- Oil (cooking oil, herbal essence oil, or frankincense)

- Black candle

Take a drop of oil on the tip of your finger and wipe it across the candle. You are going to move your finger up and down three times while saying this incantation.
Black candle, turn my luck around. Bring prosperity and joy abound.
Give your thanks and light your candle. Moving your hand to your heart chakra, you are going to say a new chant.
Flame and fire, candle burn. Work to make my luck return.
Be sure to meditate on you having good fortune and being happy while the bad luck is lifted off your shoulders and banished. Should you decide to keep the candle, you are going to need to make sure that you do not use it for any spell that is not a luck spell. This is because it is charged with a particular energy that should not be transferred off to other spells.

Reversal Spell

In using this spell, you are going to be reversing any bad luck that may be placed on you.

What you need:

- Spoon

- Your circle

- Bowl

- A white candle

- Rosemary

- Basil

- Pepper

- Cinnamon

- Mustard

- Garlic

Mix all the spices you gathered together in your bowl. Light your candle. Think of the bad luck spell that may be placed on you to make it vanish off of you. Light the spices on fire. Once they begin to smell, toss them away. Blow your candle out and ground any extra energy you may have. You are now free to close your circle.

Luck for a Day

Need just a little bit of additional luck for the big meeting that you are having or the exam that is coming up? This is a good spell for you.

What you need:

- Chamomile tea

- Belief

- Cabbage leaf

- Clover leaf

- Alfalfa leaf

If getting alfalfa is difficult for you, you can still do the spell. Ground up the leaves well. After they are ground up (you may want to make sure there are no big chunks left) sprinkle a little bit into tea.

You will say this incantation over the tea:

Fortuna, Tyche, Goddess of luck. Award me your guiding hand for one day, so I may succeed. You are a glory, the maker of luck. Support me, though I do not deserve to be in your proximity. So mote it be.

Once you have finished your spell, drink your tea and ensure you drink all of it. Also, make sure that you say thanks to the Goddess even if you do not feel as if you are having good luck that day.

Easy Luck Spell

What you need:

- Your voice

Say the following chant:

The winds of change I feel tonight,

The waters are calm, and the sky is bright,

Luck be mine, come into me,

My desires are true, so mote it be.

Luck powder

What you need:
- Calamus (1 part)

- Vetivert (2 parts)

- Nutmeg (1 part)

- Allspice (2 parts)

Mix all your herbs together. Next, sprinkle the powder around your home or around your desk at work.

Triple Gemstone Luck Spell

This spell should be done whenever the moon is waxing.
What you need:
- Frankincense incense stick

- Small wooden box that has a lid

- Green candle (1)

- Gemstones (3)

- Pen (green)

- Piece of paper

Cast your circle while you prepare your altar for the spell. Get all other thoughts out of your mind so you can focus on the task at hand. Putting both hands on the box, say the following:
By the powers of the earth,
By the powers of the air,
By the powers of the fire,
By the powers of the water,
I empower this spell box
This will assist me in my spells.

So mote it be.

Light your green candle and then your incense. Now with your paper, write down a paragraph about something good that has happened in your life. Relive that memory in your head and allow the joy that you felt at the time to flood through your body.

With each of your gemstones in hand, you are going to repeat this incantation:

Powers and energies
Send good luck my way.

Now put each gemstone into your box. Blow your candle out. Over the course of seven days, you are going to repeat the steps listed above. After seven days, you will open your box for an hour to release the energy that has become trapped inside. When you want to attract good luck, carry the stones with you.

Chapter 19: Spells for Dreams and Wishes

Dreams and wishes are part of everyday life. There are some dreams and wishes for which we just need that bit of an extra push to make it come true or to where we can make our dream or wish a bit more clear so we know exactly what we want.

Wish Spell

It is best that you do this spell before you go to bed.

What you need:

- Pen

- Candle

- Piece of paper

The color of your candle needs to match what you wish for. The candle needs to be a candle that has never been used before. Make sure your wish is clear. After you have worked all the details out in your wish, write it down on a piece of paper. Place your candle on top of the paper where your wish is located.

Clear your mind so you are not sending mixed signals into the universe. Lighting the candle, you need to only be thinking of your wish and   how it is going to look when it comes true. Allow for the realization of that wish to permeate all of your senses as if it has already come true.

Take about ten minutes to visualize this before taking that same piece of paper from under the candle and burning it.

Repeat the following:

Candle shining in the night
With your flame enchanted,

By the powers of magic might
May my wish be granted.
When the candle sheds its gleam
At the mystic hour,
Let fulfillment of my dream
Gather secret power.
Flame of magic, brightly burn,
Spirit of the fire.
Let the wheel of fortune turn,
Grant me my desire,
One, two, three – so mote it be!

A Simple Wishing Spell with Incense

If you are in a hurry, then this is a good wishing spell for you. You are going to want to do it when the moon is either waxing or full.
What you need:

- -a stick of incense of your choice

- An incense burner

Your mind should go into a state of meditation as you light a stick of incense. Moving your focus to your heart, you should feel as if you are being filled with joy. Here is where you will begin to imagine what you are wishing for to come true.

You want to imagine as much detail as possible to avoid mixed signals. You should also think of it as if it has already happened. Focus on how you are going to feel once the wish has come to pass.

Once you have gotten yourself into a spot where you can actually believe that your wish has come true, say the following chant ten times:

Magic herbs burn in fire,

Bring me my heart's desire.

Dream Spell

This spell will best be used when you are trying to enchant your dreams. You may also find this spell allows you to dream walk, but that is no guarantee. There are no special objects that are required to do this spell. Repeat this incantation:

Lady of the night,

Bless my soul with your light.

Queen of the moon,

Let your magic fill my room.

Silver dust of the bright stars,

Heal my wounds, erase my scars,

Let me wander into your realm free,

Nurture my body like a healthy tree.

Career Spell

Your job is a major aspect of your life and if you are not doing what you love, why are you doing it? Use this spell to be able to find the perfect job for you or to get your foot in the door towards getting the job of your dreams.

What you need

- A candle (green)

- Pin

Carve the title or type of job that you are seeking. Light the candle and say the following spell:

To do for me this deed

Bring to me this job I need

Your candle needs to burn out on its own, so ensure it is in a safe place where it cannot be knocked over.

Chapter 20: Spells for Health and Wellness

Our health is very important. If we are not healthy, then we are not going to be able to keep going with our lives which is not ideal. There are times a bit of help is needed when it comes to making sure we stay healthy.

Simple Health Blessing

Everything that is used in this spell is not supposed to be used as a medical cure. They are simply objects that symbolize health and vitality.

What you need:

- Candle (white)

- Glass of apple juice (organic if possible)

- Cinnamon stick

Put your juice in your glass, stir it around four times with the cinnamon stick. Set fire to the candle. Drink a little bit of the juice. Say the following incantation:

Goddess bless body and soul
Health and wellness is my goal
Drink the rest of the juice and then blow your candle out.
At any time that you feel like you may be getting sick, you can do this spell. Or, if you want to ward off any illness before it comes on, drink it every morning.

Happiness Candle Spell

Your mental status is just as important as your physical health. If you are not content, then you are not going to do the things you want to do. This spell is going to assist in bringing some joy to your life.

What you need:

- Dried lavender

- Candles (Orange, 2)

Taking the lavender, place it on your altar between your candles. Light your candles, hold your hands up   to   feel the warmth of the flame. Say this incantation seven times in a row.

This spell, please bless

For my happiness

Allow the candles to burn down on their own. Feel happiness spreading through your body as the flame that had just been burning.

Confidence Candle

How you view yourself is a big part of how you live your life. With this spell, you are going to gain a little insight on how to love yourself.

What you need:
- Pure water

- Pink candle

- Rose petals (red and white)

- Rainwater is ideal for this spell but if that is not something that you feel comfortable doing you should buy a bottle of spring water. Try and avoid using tap water unless you absolutely have to.

On your altar, take the flower petals and make a ring around your candle. Before lighting the candle, think of a few of your best qualities and meditate on those. Now that you have those thoughts in mind, you can light your candle and say the following spell:

May my own light shine
With love divine.

After you have said your spell, you are going to drink the water to rid yourself of any negative thoughts that you have in your head. Allow the candle to burn out on its own.

Healing Candle Spell

What you need:
- Light blue candles (3)

- Pin

Carve your name or the name of the person you are casting the spell for into the candles. Place the candles in their holders on your altar. Light your candles and then say this incantation:

Healing light

Shine tonight

The power I feel

Be used to heal

Meditate on the condition that needs to be healed. The candles should be allowed to burn out on their own.

Simple Motivation Incantation

As mentioned in a previous spell, your mental health is just as important to your well-being as your physical health. This is a spell that does not require you to gather any objects together, all you are going to need to do is say the following incantation to improve your motivation so that you can get things done.

Speak these words whenever you feel like your motivation is lacking and you need to get a task done:

May these words bring me comfort

And rekindle my interest in this moment,

I invoke the higher power.

Among the hindrances these hours

To rouse the motivation in my heart.

As visions of great return,

And the spark of positivity is lit,

And the strength rises within me.

It is my wish; please guide my steps

During this moment.

May this incantation

Push me forward,

So mote it be.

A Spell to Increase Patience

It is easy to find yourself being impatient throughout the day, but being impatient does not do you any good as you have most likely found out. So, why not bring a little more patience into your life so things go smoother throughout the day whenever it comes to dealing with other people, whether they be at home or work.

What you need:

- Essential oil (palmarosa, lavender, jasmine)

- A cup of water

- A candle (blue)

Be sure to cast your circle before you light your candle. Focus on the flame as you take in around ten deep breaths so you can steady yourself. Each time that you breathe in think about inhaling the peaceful blue of the candle. Every time that you exhale think of all your frustrations and impatience being lifted out of your body and taken away from you.

Once you have finished your breathing, you will move on to the cup of water. Three drops of the oil that you have chosen should be dropped into the water. After you have done this, you will place your fingertips in the water and stir it while saying:

Blessed waters cool my spirit,

Fill me with your soothing peace.

Like the river, I shall flow

Patiently, with joy and ease.

At this point, you can close your circle and blow out your candle. Be sure to keep the cup of water on your altar so when you begin to feel impatient, you can inhale the water and redo your spell.

Spell to Restore Health and Vigor

After you say this chant, you should begin to feel refreshed. What you need:

- Your voice

Say this chant or something similar to it:

Sky above me stars so bright

Hear my plea upon this night,

Restore health and vigor in me,

The spell is done, so mote it be!

Health Spell

Everyone wants to be healthy and have their loved ones healthy. But, you cannot ask for health in a spell, you need to ask for the tools that are required in making sure you can stay healthy or become healthy. No one's health should be placed in jeopardy when this spell is done lest it comes back to you threefold.

What you need:

- Teaspoon of lavender flowers

- Glass of moon water (full moon)

- Lavender scented candle

- Quartz crystal (clear)

Dim the lights and center yourself. Boil the moon water, do not do anything with it until it is at a full boil. Drop in the flowers. As you breathe in the steam and scent, you need to repeat this saying:

Purple flowers heal my head; I will not take to my bed. The pain will flee oh rising steam, take the pain with thee.

After saying this, strain the liquid into a cup and sit down to sip the tea. Let the warmth of the tea overcome your boy as your headache becomes calmed. After one sip, you will place the crystal over the remaining liquid and repeat the rest of the spell:

Crystal bright, bring your shining light. Take this pain to keep me sane. Right now I feel no mirth. Your power is from the earth. Send this pain away and make my day.

Place the crystal over your third eye. Lay down and allow the crystal to take away the pain. Now wash it in the sink under running water as you imagine your pain going down the drain.

Depression Banishment

In modern times, it is hard to find someone that does not

suffer from some sort of depression. You do not want to allow depression to take over your life and a good way to do this is to use this spell while you focus on the good that is in your life. It is hard to do this sometimes, but keep trying. You are strong!

What you need:

- 2 candles (pink and yellow)

Light your candles and repeat the following words:

Blessed Goddess of love and light

Please come help me on this night.

My heart is heavy, and my feelings are blue,

My soul is sad I do not know what to do...

Help me banish the pain I feel,

This lackluster feeling has no appeal.

Help me see the love begin and

Feel my heart be light again,

Let me climb up from this hole,

And be with you heart, body and soul.

I ask thee Goddess on this night, please

Help me make myself alright!

So mote it be!

Chapter 21: Money Spells

Money is hard to get and even harder to keep. We all need it to survive, and some need it more than others depending on their situation. However, we all need it, and there never seems to be enough to go around. With these few simple spells, you can hopefully get some of that green that you need.

Pagan Money Attraction Spell

What you need:

- Silk or cord colored green or gold (13 inches)
- Green candle (1)

Tie a knot in the cord you have while saying this spell:

With knot one, this spell has started.

With knot two, plenty of tasks to do.

With knot three, wealth comes to me.

With knot four, opportunity is tapping on my door.

With knot five, I am and will succeed.

With knot six, financial problems will be fixed.

With knot seven, success will follow.

With knot eight, increase is great.

With knot nine, all of this is mine.

The best time to do this spell is either during a full moon or a waxing moon as you are trying to increase your financial holdings.

Money Wish Spell

This spell is best done on a Thursday, Friday or Sunday of a full moon or a waxing moon.

What you need:

- Visualization skills that are honed in and powerful

- A special coin or something you consider a good luck charm

Visualize yourself with the amount of money you need. Be sure to visualize yourself receiving this money. The more you visualize, the more charge your coin is going to have.

As you clutch the coin in your hand, say this chant or something similar to it:

Silver and gold, return unto me

By the witchy powers of three hundred times three

The money I require is mine to keep

Make your way to me, immediately.

Keep this coin with you and forget about the spell.

You can give thanks to the Goddess or the universe at the end of your spell if you want to. It is a personal option. However, it is highly recommended that you give thanks to your goddess so that she knows that she is appreciated for helping you.

Everything Under the Moon Money Spell

This money spell should be done under a full moon on a Thursday if possible.

Before you do this spell, meditate and try and forget about your money problems or else you are going to end up causing the spell to go astray. It is best that you are not in desperate need for money.

You need to do the spell and forget about it with the faith that the Goddess and God are going to provide for you as they see fit.

What you need:
- Silver coins

- Cauldron

- Water

- Candles (1 white and 1 green)

Place the water in your cauldron until it is about half full. Toss the silver coin into the cauldron, quarters usually work best. Put the cauldron near a window so that it can absorb the moonlight. As you glide your hand over the surface, think of it as you are trying to pick up the silver that is reflecting off the surface of the moon.

Chant the following:

Lovely lady of the moon, deliver to me your wealth right soon. Fill my hands with silver and gold. All you give me, my pockets can hold.

You are going to want to repeat this spell three times.

Step away from the bowl and leave it there for the entire night so that it gets all of the moonbeams. Upon waking up the next morning, dump the water out into the earth but be sure not to put the coins with it.

Grow Some Wealth

What you need :
- Dried patchouli (sprinkling)

- A houseplant (one that is thriving is best)

- A coin

It does not matter what kind of plant you get. However, basil plants work best. Put a little bit of the patchouli into the soil but not enough to choke the plant off from water. Taking the coin, stick it into the soil as well, but leave part of it out where you can see it.

Should you get some money, you are going to want to spend the coin in the soil as soon as possible, replacing it with a different coin. Continue the process until you believe you are satisfied.

Spice Up Your Wallet

This spell is very simple and is going to be used so you can get some extra money in your life.

What you need:
- A paper money

- Ground cinnamon

Pick a Thursday and rub the cinnamon on your fingers. Taking the fingers with cinnamon on them, leave five different smudge marks on the bill. Place this bill into the space where you keep your money. Leaving it there is going to attract new wealth.

A Simple Prosperity Spell

The purpose of this spell is to assist in bringing some inner peace and prosperity to your life.

What you need:

- Cinnamon (a pinch)

- Bundle of sage (1)

- A bowl

- Green candle

Light your candle on your altar. Take your sage and sprinkle some on the flame as well as around the candle. Think only of positive things such as achieving inner peace and prosperity. Watch your flame grow before you start to sprinkle your cinnamon on your flame saying this incantation:

I embrace prosperity and inner peace.

Your candle should be allowed to burn out on its own. Once the flame is extinguished, bury it so that your spell can be manifested into reality

Spell for Money or Prosperity

Money is the root of all evil, or so we've been told. But, money is needed to ensure that you can take care of yourself or your loved ones. With this spell, you are going to raise your prosperity so you can gain more money and be able to survive in a world that revolves around money.

What you need:

- Caldron with burning coals

- Athame or a wand

- Water

- Dish of salt or soil

- Sage

- Basil

- Chamomile

You will want to do this during a waxing moon on a Sunday or a Thursday.

Cast your circle. Invite your deity to your circle. Put the herbs that you have gathered into the burning coals as you visualize your goal. Sprinkle just a few drops of water and salt on the charcoal.

As you move your wand or athame over the cauldron, be sure to go in a clockwise motion while saying your spell:

By the abilities of air, fire, water, and earth. I release this spell. I ask for divine supervision as I seek help this day. With harm to none, this spell be fulfilled.

Continue to meditate on your goal while you imagine the smoke taking the energy out of your circle and spreading it throughout the universe. Thank your deity for their help in the spell. Release your circle. Center yourself before you leave your circle.

Chapter 22: Other Helpful Spells

These spells will be helpful to you but cannot be put into a specific category. If you place these spells in your Book of Shadows, you may discover you will have to make a tab that is special to miscellaneous spells.

Finding What Has Been Lost

It does not matter how long or short your spell is, if you put your entire heart into it then it is going to bring you the results that you are looking for.

With this spell, you are going to be trying to locate something that you may have misplaced in your home.

What you need:

- A white candle

Light your candle and place it on something that is going to be easy to carry around without dropping.

Walk room to room saying this incantation:

I need what I seek

Give me a peek

Draw my eyes

For my prize.

As you go into a room and say your incantation, look around the room so you can see if you are feeling drawn to where the object may be located.

Hushed Moment

Whenever some peace is needed in your life so you can smooth out what is happening around you, this spells is one that you can use.

What you need:
- White thread (several inches long)

- White feather (1)

You need a quiet place to do this spell, even if that means that you lock yourself in the bathroom to do it. Tie the feather to it to the white thread, but do not use all of the string for this. Hold the end that is not holding the feather and place the feather in front of your face. Breath out and watch as the feather swings until it comes to rest.

As the feather is swinging, whisper these words:

Still, quiet, hush

I am not in a rush.

You are going to repeat your spell once again after the feather has come to rest.

Altar Dedication

After you have your altar setup, you will need to cleanse the space so that it becomes dedicated to your magic work only.

What you need:

- Ritual tools (The tools that were discussed in a previous chapter. These tools are optional)

- Altar candles (2)

- White candle

- Incense

Burn a little bit of incense around your altar to ensure that the space is cleansed. The candles should be placed on opposite ends of your altar. As you begin your spell, light the candle that is on the left before lighting the one that is on the right. Lastly, light the white candle before picking it up.

Walking clockwise around the space that is set up for your altar, you are going to say this chant:

By the light, which cuts through darkness

By the fire, which burns within

By my will, which stirs the elements

Let nothing harmful in.

Upon the completion of your circle, place your candle in front of the altar before saying the end of the spell:

So mote it be.

With your space dedicated, you can do any spells or cleansings that you need to do. Once you have finished, you need to   take the white candle up once more and walk the opposite direction while saying your spell

By my will, which called the elements.

By the fire, which burned so bright.

By the light, which lit the darkness

I leave you for tonight.

Blow your candle out. Extinguish the other candles first right then left. Finish off by saying:

So mote it be.

Calming Spell

It is hard to calm down once you have gotten yourself worked up or if you just feel as though you need a little bit of support. With this spell, you are going to be able to find the calm that you need.

What you need:

- Noise of some kind of keep you calm such as white noise or classical music (or silence if you prefer)

- Crystal (amethyst is good for calming rituals)

- A bowl filled with water

- A candle (color choice is yours)

- Incense or oil in a scent that is appealing to you or is associated with your intent

Light your candle along with your incense if you are using some. Ensure there is clean water in your bowl before placing your crystal in it. Work towards clearing your mind of the chaotic thoughts that may be swirling around your head and focus on positive calming thoughts. Once you have control of your thoughts, project your calmness to the water so that it may absorb that calming energy.

At the point in time that you feel like you have gotten enough calming energy into the crystal that you are using, you will remove the crystal from the water. If you have chosen to use oils, dab a little bit of oil on your rock. If you are using incense, hold your rock over the smoke so that it may absorb the smell that you associate with being calm. The last thing you do is hold your crystal over the flame of your candle for it to dry.

Keep your crystal with you, and at any point in time that you begin to feel anxious you can hold it or rub it in order to feel the calm energy that was absorbed into it through your ritual.

Full Body Blessing

In doing this spell, you are going to be connecting your physical body to your spirit as well as opening up your readiness channel. You will need to do this during a full moon so that you can see the moon.

What you need:

- Pine incense

- White candle

- Sandalwood incense

- Bowl of water

- Pinch of salt

Light your candle and incense. Sprinkle the salt into the water. Standing at your altar, you will touch each part of your body saying the following:

Eyes: bless my eyes that I might have clarity of vision.

Mouth: bless my mouth that I may speak the truth.

Ears: bless my ears that I may hear all that is spoken and not.

Heart: anoint my heart that I may be saturated with love.

Feet: bless my feet that I may find and walk my own true path.

Allow yourself to be filled with the understanding and love being offered from the Goddess After you are done, you will extinguish your candle and let your incense burn down. You will want to dump the water into the earth so that any negative energy it may have captured is released back into the earth.

Wand Blessing

A wand is not a required tool for doing your spells and rituals. However, it is something that you may decide to use from time to time. If you elect to use a wand, you are going to want to bless it so it can be blessed, charged and ready for its intended purpose.

What you need:

- Your wand

Holding your wand, say the following incantation to charge it so you can use it for your spells:

Through the strength of the elements

Light of the sun, empower this wand.

Splendor of fire, empower this wand.

Speed of lighting, empower this wand.

Swiftness of wind, empower this wand.

Depth of the seas, empower this wand.

Stability of the earth, empower this wand.

Firmness of rock, empower this wand.

I charge and empower this wand.

So mote it be.

Chapter 23: Tips and Tricks

Tips and tricks are going to make your spells that much easier. Learning which spells work for you and which ones do not will be a journey and will be one you will have to take on your own.

However, it is a great idea to have some advice or some tips and tricks from fellow Wiccans. Don't forget to share with other Wiccans so you can help make their journey a little easier.

- Salt: Placing a circle of salt around an area helps to prevent negative entities and demons from entering that space. You may also use salt to make a line on doors or window sills so that they become impassable to malicious spirits.

- Iron: Iron helps to repel evil which is why Wiccans place an iron object at the entrance of their home to deter any unwanted visitors. Hammering three iron nails into the frame of a window or door (1 at each side on the bottom and 1 at the top in the middle) will help to keep malevolent spirits from entering the home. It is believed that most spirits cannot cross railway lines since the iron creates an impenetrable wall for them.

- Silver: Silver is a symbol for the moon and the Goddess. Using silver for jewelry makes it easier to enchant as a talisman for protection. Silver pentagrams are powerful objects of protection even without having a spell placed on them.

- The pentacle: A five pointed star that symbolizes the five elements and can be traced anywhere as a symbol of protection.

- Light: Lesser demons typically avoid any area that is bright and will only attack when it is dark. However, this does not work for demons who are of higher rank.

- Fire: There are some spirits that are afraid of fire, especially those that are related to ice or water. This is what makes a candle a tool for protection.

- Crystals: Quartz crystals that are blessed by a witch can help to create a circle of protection. Arrange them in a circle so spirits find it hard to cross. The circle can protect you or can be used to trap spirits in the middle. The circle will be stronger if the crystals are placed at the cardinal points.

- Gemstones: Stones and gems are going to be very useful in magic and can be used for protection. Tiger's eye will reflect negative energies while amethyst blocks any manipulative spirits and helps to decrease the effects of harmful potions. Magnetite can entrap lesser demons and opal can lock higher demons up for a short period of time. Onyx and obsidian are able to cancel out various negative energies like necromancy. The mineral that is used most often is a clear quartz, but it has to be blessed first to be effective.

- Orgonite: This is an energy healing tool that is usually made up of resin, gemstones and metals. It can be used in re-balancing negative energies. There are a lot of people who use orgonite for protection against any harmful electromagnetic pollution. It can also be used for powerful spiritual protection.

- Incense: There is a great variety of incense that can be used to repel negative energy. If you have the proper quality incense, you will be able to keep them away.

Some of the most common protection incense are sage, sandalwood, frankincense, patchouli and myrrh.

- Plants: There are several spices and herbs that have protection qualities. Garlic is able to repel any creature that drains their victims. Saffron and thyme deter flying spirits that are usually tied to the wind. Rosemary repels evil spirits linked to water. Sage, when it is burnt, is cleansing and intolerable to any negative spirit. Henbane and aconite repels demons violently because they are extremely toxic, which means that you have to be careful when you handle them. Lilacs, when they are planted near the house, will deter any wandering spirit who passes by. The branches of a thorny plant like a rose can be as effective as a salt line when placed along a door or window sill. Myrrh helps to strengthen any spell or protective talisman.

- Athame: Most Wiccans do not sharpen their athame because it is never used to cut anything. However, because it is a knife, it should be handled with caution. The athame is a phallic symbol which makes it a symbol of the God. Athames that have been blessed properly can be used to draw a circle of protection. Point it in the air and draw your circle's boundaries. On top of that, the atame can hurt demons and spirits despite the fact that they have no physical body.

- Broom: This is a symbol for cleaning and brooms that are placed at doors prevent weaker spirits from entering. Should a dangerous spirit enter the house, brooms will fall to the ground as an alarm signal.

- Dig deep: Before you start planning what you want manifested, you have to dig deep. This will apply if you are asking for something that you have not gotten before.

For example, if you constantly ask for an apartment or job, but despite your wishing you continue to run into roadblocks, you probably feel as if you are not being listened to. Remember that the universe will provide you with anything that you want, you may just not know exactly what you want.
You have to be careful what you wish for because once you get it, you may not want it after all. Keep in mind that everything has 2 sides which is why you must explore the downsides to the wish that you are asking for.

- Imagine: Imagine how your life will be once you get what you wish for. There are often things that hold you back, one of the biggest things that will hold you back is the feeling that you have to have everything planned out while still wanting mystery. You have to be willing to let go and allow the universe to flow through you as it is supposed to.

- The power of three: Before you start manifesting what you want, you have to ask if it is going to harm anyone or yourself? If it could potentially harm you or someone else, you should not try to manifest your wish.

Chapter 24: Wiccan Myths Debunked

As you know, there are a lot of myths about the Wiccan religion. In this chapter, we will debunk some of the myths that people commonly believe.

- Wiccans are witches: This is true. However, Wicca is different from witchcraft. Witchcraft is the practice and belief of magic while Wicca is based in nature. Each will compliment each other, not every Wiccan practices magic while not all witches are Wiccan. There are even some in other religions that have been known to practice magic.

- Wiccans use magic to hurt people: Sadly, this is true. There are some spells that have the ability to cause others harm in some way. However, not every Wiccan is out to get those that are not in the religion.

In fact, as you have seen, the first rule is "harm none, do what you will." Basically, this means that Wiccans are usually peaceful people. When you combine this with the rule of three, Wiccans know that when they go out of their way to harm someone, they will eventually receive a worse treatment. This is why when most Wiccans cast spells to harm someone else, they only do it out of self-defense or to right a wrong.

- Wiccans worship the devil: This is the furthest thing from the truth. The idea of satan came from the Christian religion which is why it does not make sense for Wiccans to worship satan. They also believe that the pentagram is an image associated with the devil. However, it's Greek roots come from Pan and is used as a symbol for protection and magical energy.

- Wiccans are always naked and participate in unsafe sex: False! There are a few ceremonies that Wiccans have where they participate in nudity, but they do not walk around naked like nudists do. For their nude ceremonies, they find a secluded place where they can practice in peace. There are some Wiccans that view sex as a celebration of fertility and life but they practice safe and private sex just like everyone else.

- Wicca is a cult: Wrong! It is a religion. Yes, like every other religion, there are those that are considered "weird." The only reason people believe that Wicca is a cult is because they are mysterious and often practice in secret.

- Wiccans have sex orgies: Not even close. Even though some Wiccans are liberal about their sexuality, they do not participate in orgies. Everyone in the Wiccan religion is an adult so they do not care if you are gay, straight or polyamourous.

- Do Wiccans cast spells?: Yes! As you've seen in this book, there are a number of spells that a Wiccan can cast to manifest their wishes. This is not Harry Potter magic. There are some spells that are nothing more than prayers sent up to the gods while others are going to be based on your intent.

- What is the difference between Wiccan and pagan? Almost every Wiccan is pagan, but not all pagans are Wiccans. In other words, pagan is an umbrella term for a group of different spiritual paths.

- Why do people want to become Wiccan? There are a number of reasons that people decide to become Wiccan. Some want to become Wiccan because they are not happy with any other religion. Others decide to study various religions and decide that Wiccan is the one that is most compatible with their beliefs. No matter what their reason, every Wiccan says they chose this path because it was what was right for them.

- How are new Wiccans recruited: They aren't! The information is shared with those who want the answers, but Wicca does not recruit people into the religion. Wiccans only want those that truly want to be in the religion on their side.

- Are you worried about going to hell? No, as you saw earlier, Satan is a concept from the Christian religion so is Hell. This is why they do not worry about going to hell because they focus on the good things as they believe that what is done in this lifetime will echo upon the next one.

- Do you believe in God? Most Wiccans are polytheistic which means that they believe in more than one deity.

- You have to come from a family of witches: Having a family member that is in the religion will help you, but that is not required. There are many people that make the decision to become Wiccan because their beliefs line up with the beliefs of the Wiccan religion.

- You have to be initiated in order to become a witch: Nope! If you decide to join a coven, then you will be forced to go through initiation so you can show how much you know about their traditions. But, for informal witches, you can mark your progress with a small ritual.

- You have to cast spells naked: Some people choose to cast them naked, but this is not required. If it is part of a festival then you may cast them naked. However, if you are in a coven and they are advocating that you do something that makes you uncomfortable, you should leave it. You should never feel coerced to do something that you do not believe is in your best interest.

There are a million different myths that have been put out there by those that do not understand the religion. If you are serious about wanting to join the religion, if you have not already, it is best for you to find someone that can help you to understand what you do not understand. It is always a good idea for you to understand everything before you jump head first into the Wiccan religion.

Conclusion

If you are just starting out with Wicca, then this book hopefully helped you figure out where to get your start. Herbal magic and moon magic are going to be the easiest places to start. Once you are able to harness the power you can gain from those, then you will be ready to move on to more complicated spells.

If you are a practicing Wiccan and were looking to expand your skills, then I hope that this book was able to show you a new magic that you may not have thought about before.

The Wiccan religion is extremely fascinating and there is always something else that you can learn about it. Not only that, but the Wiccan beliefs can help you to feel as if you are in control of your life and that you are able to keep going when you feel like you can't go anymore. This is thanks to the spells you can perform or the support system you'll get from a coven.

The hope is that no matter what level of Wiccan you are, you are able to take what you learned in this book and put it to good use. And remember, no matter what you do, do no harm!

Blessed Be! And good luck on your journey.

CPSIA information can be obtained
at www.ICGtesting.com
Printed in the USA
BVHW041400270421
605944BV00006B/1186

9 781802 290332